LIFE ON THE STAND

LIFE ON THE STAND

Memoir of an Artist Model

HELENE SIMKIN JARA

Helene Simkin Jara

Contents

	Dedication	x
	What People Are Saying	xi
I	The Auditions	1
II	The Models Guild	6
III	Now What?	8
IV	What Are Models Like?	11
V	Where Did This All Start?	12
VI	Acting in New York City	14
VII	Night on a Subway	30
VIII	Pathway from Theater to Artist Model	33
IX	Improv Troupe in Silverlake	36
X	Modeling in Southern California and Los Angeles	42
XI	Santa Monica	48
XII	Modeling with Someone Else	53
XIII	Glad to See a Cop	57
XIV	Racism	60

XV	Student Passed Out	62
XVI	Is She Smiling?	64
XVII	Up on a Rock in L.A.	66
XVIII	Perspective	68
XIX	Modeling for Each Other in Santa Monica	71
XX	Anton - Atypical Hookup	74
XXI	Learning While Modeling	78
XXII	Beginning Artists	79
XXIII	A Booking Worth Forgetting	80
XXIV	Art Teachers' Styles	81
XXV	What It Takes	83
XXVI	Expectations	85
XXVII	Kinds of Poses and Preferences	87
XXVIII	Musing While on the Stand	89
XXIX	Modeling in the Bay Area	106
XXX	Ford	108
XXXI	The Guild and Flo Allen	110
XXXII	Katy and Nancy in Noe Valley	113
XXXIII	The Redheads	125
XXXIV	Who Would Do That?	130
XXXV	Stars and Stripes Knee Socks	132
XXXVI	Artists in the Bay Area	135

XXXVII	Meeting Franklin Williams	139
XXXVIII	Monkey Shit	145
XXXIX	Shit that Happens	146
XL	Some Hazards of Being a Model	148
XLI	Taking an Unauthorized Booking	151
XLII	Bugs	153
XLIII	Dogs	154
XLIV	Other Hazards	156
XLV	Fetishes	158
XLVI	Artistic Whims	161
XLVII	Fake Zits	162
XLVIII	Fetishes in Berkeley	163
XLIX	Unfortunate Bodily Functions	165
L	Interviews with Infamous Artist Models from the '70s	167
LI	Boom Boom	179
LII	Poems about Modeling	185
LIII	Contemporary Artist Model Interview 2021	187
LIV	A Few Art Teachers' Stories	190
LV	Speedo or Not?	193
LVI	Linda Levy's Nasty Stories	195
LVII	Full Circle	200

LVIII	Moving On	206

About The Author   209
Special Thanks!   211

Copyright © 2022 by Helene Simkin Jara

All rights reserved. No part of this book may be reproduced in any manner whatsoever without written permission except in the case of brief quotations embodied in critical articles and reviews.

First Printing, 2022

Writing a memoir about being an artist model
is just like *being* an artist model.

It's all there.

What People Are Saying

Helene Simkin Jara is a cool cat. Her Fellini film of a memoir is pure reading pleasure, a wild romp through the world of artists models in San Francisco in the free fall, free form years just after the Summer of Love. The voice is wan and sexy, the alert eye always ready to wink. But for all the over-the-top fun (Please, more Boom-Boom!), there is a more profound message lurking underneath: sometimes the object of your gaze is no object, but an alert intelligence sizing you up in turn.

Steve Kettmann
Author of *One Day at Fenway, Remember Who You Are, Letter to the New President,* Co-director of Wellstone Center in the Redwoods.

~~~

Helene Simkin Jara's musings on her days in the theater and modeling are funny and touching, a truly delightful read.

Clifford Mae Henderson
Improv artist, author of five award-winning novels, including *Perfect Little Worlds,* and *Things I'm Thinking About.*

~~~

What happens when a creative soul whose default response to the world is "Yes!" signs up to be a nude model? 'Life on the Stand' is a lively, funny, head-spinning account of Helene Simkin Jara's experiences as an artists model in the hedonistic, let-it-all-hang-out era of the 1970s. The author takes us all on a wild romp from New York to

Los Angeles to Big Sur to the capitals of Europe before landing in San Francisco. In the process, she introduces us to a parade of eccentric, often unforgettable characters in the outlandish and spirited world of artists and models. The result is a whirlwind of a memoir that is — to borrow one such character's assessment of the kind of people who become artists models — 'crazy, demented, flamboyant, and exhibitionistic.'

Wallace Baine
Author of *A Light in the Midst of Darkness: The Story of a Bookshop, a Community* and *True Love.*

~~~

Life On The Stand takes readers into the fascinating world of artist models and Helene Simkin Jara gets naked both literally and figuratively in this compelling memoir. The stories range from amusing, to shocking, to terrifying. From Southern California to Europe to Morocco—get ready for the ride of your life—and answers to the questions you didn't know you had. Was there really a union for Artist Model's in San Francisco? What were the auditions like? How does it feel to be nude with someone else on a model stand while people draw, paint or sculpt you? Do models watch the artists? What are their inner fantasies? Helene is a powerful writer with a story to tell!

Lara Love Hardin
CEO of Idea Architects, Co-author of the NYT bestseller *The Sun Does Shine*, Author of the forthcoming memoir, *The Neighbor From Hell & Other People I Have Been.*

I

The Auditions

I was determined to get the hell away from L.A. for good, and being a model in San Francisco could be my ticket out.

I had heard that San Francisco Models Guild had auditions coming up. I had also heard lots of rumors that the union was falling apart and wasn't much help to its members. I decided to audition anyway. These were huge, scary tryouts where they only accepted a few people. But as an actor with lots of theater experience, I was used to rejection. I thought to myself, *I know I'm a good model. What can I lose?* I might as well go through with it. If I get in, fine. If I don't? Plan B. Whatever that is.

I drove up from L.A. in seven hours—pretty good timing. By the time I had arrived in San Francisco, I was tired and spacey from driving—but after getting lost as usual, I managed to find the San Francisco Art Institute. Once at the school, I didn't need to bother asking if I was in the right place. All I had to do was follow the weird bunch of people heading in the same direction. I assumed we were all at the Art Institute for the same purpose. Or maybe all San Franciscans looked like this? It was 1972.

There were about seventy people in the corridor waiting to audition. We were each given a number, and then we were invited into a big room, to see a demonstration about what the judges would expect from us. Then, we heard a little story about the San Francisco Models Guild. After being herded into the room, we sat, or stood, against the walls, facing four women and one man. One of the four women, I would find out later, was the booking agent, Nancy. The other four were models. Katy, the most voluminous one, was the president of the Guild, and David (aka Boom Boom) was a well-known model.

Two women showed us the first pose. Susan was tall, blonde and lanky; Katy was round and weighed over 250 pounds. Susan sat on a chair above Katy, who was sitting on the model's stand, hung her long slender legs over Katy's shoulders, while both women formed triangles with their arms over their heads. When they had finished showing us their examples of short and long poses, there was a great silence in the room. I mean, how could any of us, posing alone, live up to those two? The juxtaposition of the angular lines of Susan and the very round ones of Katy was magnificent.

One of the female judges was sitting in a wheelchair. I thought to myself that San Francisco was certainly progressive, if they used models with physical disabilities.

As I was standing in line, I looked around at my competition. There was a platinum blonde waiting to audition who had stars painted on her forehead and cheeks— the kind teachers used to put on your spelling test if you got 100%. What else could embellish a woman wearing open-toed, gold-lamé, high-heeled shoes with a turquoise kimono, slightly opened, revealing flames painted from her shaved pubis to her bellybutton? She looked like Jean Harlow with melon-shaped breasts, black fingernail polish, and bee-stung lips with ruby-red lipstick. And then, there was the guy wearing devil's horns and a sequined G-string that had a hole in the center for his penis.

A lot of the people waiting to audition were doing yoga and breathing exercises. There I was with my jeans, tennies and white peasant blouse. The only thing it seemed I had going for me was blubber. We ended up pressed together at the bottom of a flight of stairs so packed with people that I couldn't see the top. Someone turned to me and asked, "Is this the line for the auditions?"

"Hope so."

A woman with black-framed glasses then informed us we were to come back in when our number was called. Thank God, my number was eight.

As I surveyed my competition, a butterfly danced in my stomach. I stood near the door and watched people as they went into the audition room and returned. It seemed to take about six or seven minutes a person. Most of them looked freaked as they entered and perplexed as they came out. Number seven seemed to take forever. She finally came back out, looking relieved. Adjusting the belt of her robe, she shrugged her shoulders, looked at me and said, "It's all yours, Honey. Good luck!"

I found myself entering the room, which suddenly appeared even larger than before. The judges were talking among themselves with their backs to me. I walked over to the woman in the wheelchair and handed her my resume. They all looked up, startled. I took a deep breath, walked across the room to the stand-alone dressing area, threw off my clothes and changed into my robe. I then walked defiantly back across the room, attempting to appear confident and professional.

The enormous woman, Katy, who had shown us the pose earlier, abruptly asked me to show them what I would do for a few 1-minute poses. These were my forte, so I felt quite confident. I threw off my robe and began with what I called my Grecian vase pose. I held my arms high in the air, framing my head. My wrists were limp, so that my hands fell gracefully with the force of gravity. I bent my knees and stuck my hips way out to the right and froze. I did a few more of my best short poses, making sure that I changed from standing to seated to reclining and also that I faced different sides of the room each time. Then, I was asked to show them an example of a 20-minute pose. I sat in the chair and swung my body upside down with my legs over the top of the chair, my arms falling onto the floor in an abandoned-looking pose.

I did a few more short examples of "20s" and then was asked to show an example of a three-hour pose. I sat on the floor with my back to them and rested my arms and my head on the seat of the chair. (I found out later that in the Guild, one was allowed a 5-minute break every twenty minutes. This helped a lot for the painting or sculpture classes where it was just one pose for the three hours. Legs were less apt to fall asleep as well.)

"Thank you," said Katy.

I stood up, aware that I had been trembling and sweating a great deal. They all had big smiles on their faces. That was promising. A man who looked like a satyr asked me if I got much work in Los Angeles. What was I supposed to say to that? I found out later he had only been trying to help me relax. But at the time, I felt like saying, "No, they hate me there. That's why I'm moving up here." I am from the East Coast; can't get rid of the sarcasm. But the judge's comment did remind me that I had a letter of recommendation from the Otis Art Institute, which I gave to the woman in the black glasses. Uncomfortable and unable to think of any witty small talk, I excused myself and left. *Well, it was over.* Now for the seven-hour drive home.

As I was walking out the door, they said I was wonderful and to call them in two days. Because I lived in L.A., they would tell me sooner than the others. When I heard from the booking agent, Nancy, I got such a positive response, I almost dropped the phone. I was in! I'd got in! I was a bona fide member of the San Francisco Models Guild. I could hardly believe it. My life was starting to look good again. I was ecstatic. Years later, when I asked why they had chosen me, Nancy teased me, telling me it was because I had curly armpit hair. She told me that the group of judges had nicknamed me Hilda Hot-to-Trot, because I was the only person in the history of the Models Guild who had brought a letter of recommendation.

II

The Models Guild

Just what kind of organization had I been accepted into? I was told that the purpose of the Guild was to provide a booking agency for professional art models in the Bay Area. It was run like any other organization. Members paid dues to cover the phone bill through which we got our jobs, and the organization had rules to protect both the models and the clients. For example, a model from the Guild was assured of a 5-minute break every twenty minutes. If the venue was too cold and a heater wasn't provided, the model didn't have to work and got paid anyway.

One way the Guild protected its members was by checking out each new job. When a new booking came in, in order to impress the hell out of the potential employer and to find out if the job was safe for the model, the Guild would send out one of their most experienced models—usually Toni Tandalayo, who could handle anything and had been around a few years. No Guild model had to worry about any job being too weird, although there had been several notable exceptions.

(We'll get into that later.) The rumors about the Guild falling apart were unjustified.

California College of Arts and Crafts (CCAC) charged an arm and a leg for students to go there, but they refused to pay the $4.50-an-hour minimum wage for the Model's Guild. We in the Guild were not allowed to work for them because of that. While CCAC had lots of classes that used models, they were not the largest employer, and most other educational or private employers did not balk at the cost. This was 1971 – 1974.

The San Francisco Model's Guild
Walter Swarthout

III

Now What?

    I was happy to have been hired into the Guild, and I would soon find out what artist models do once in a union. I'm the kind of person who just dives in. No questions asked. When I studied Theatre Arts at UCLA, we were taught to say "yes" to everything. *Can you be a dog?* "Yes!" *Can you tap dance and sing operatically?* "Yes!" *Can you change genders for the play?* "Yes!" Actually, I think this attitude was right up my alley, even before I studied theater. When I was eighteen, for example, I traveled with someone I barely knew to Big Sur, who gave me LSD, which wasn't even illegal at the time. I said, "What is this?"

    He said, "Just take it. You'll love it." I did. It turned out to be the worst and best night of my life. I saw, felt, tasted, smelled and heard my soul. I loved and hated me, and I changed from being an atheist to an agnostic that night.

    I had learned what artist models do by doing it. Models usually work for art classes, though sometimes they may be hired by private art groups or individual working artists. I worked for drawing, painting and sculpture classes and did whatever was asked of me. ("Yes!") An artist model is a vehicle for a creation. For short poses (from 30 seconds to 5 minutes long) I could get a lot of exercise. I could think of geometric patterns and change from standing to sitting to twisting. I could be a human pretzel. I learned the hard way; that to hold a longer pose (10 minutes or more), I shouldn't leave my arms in the air or put my body into an uncomfortable, if interesting, position. For the longer ones (maybe the same pose for a three-hour class with breaks every 20 minutes or so), I needed to be relaxed as possible and do one of two things: drift off into my mind or look at whomever was in my line of vision and make up little stories about who they were. If I did the latter, I would try and talk to them on my breaks and see if I was right.

Many beginning students apologize to the model for what they think was a bad drawing or painting. I learned that it took time to really "see" what one is looking at. In other words, I don't have straight hair and a ski-jump nose. My favorite classes were the ones where I was expected to have my own repertoire of poses. Unfortunately, sometimes it was brutally cold in the room with the students wearing thick jackets and expecting me to pose without a heater. *No.*

The coolest thing was when the teacher was lecturing about art history and showing slides while I was on a break. I was getting an art education and getting paid for it. During the '70s some of the teachers were inspired to use different locations other than classrooms. That was sometimes quite exhilarating and sometimes a disaster. Two instances come to mind: one where we were in a park near Los Angeles and a helicopter with police landed. Another was when I was set up in another park in southern California and a photography student from an art college decided to wrap my nude body in an American flag. That wasn't appreciated by all.

A good model is someone who knows her or his body and what it can do, who has a good sense of patterns, who can bring some creativity, either by using props (boas, hats, accessories) or by cultivating a constructive attitude at each session.

Classrooms, people's homes, and parks are a few places where I've worked. In people's homes, there might be food and wine, and it definitely was never cold. When I've seen the paintings in museums, I wonder about the models who posed for them. I wonder if the smell of the oil was the same as what I experienced, if the sounds of the pencils on the paper were similar. I've read that those models were sometimes the lovers of the artists. In my experience, that was hardly ever true.

In case you're wondering, artist models have little in common with fashion models. Artists and art students tend to be more interested in curves and rounded shapes, than in straight lines and flat planes. Most artist models I know, with the exception of a very few, look like everybody else in their street clothes. Some of them even look plain until they disrobe. It is then that their beauty and grace get revealed.

In Repose
Anonymous

IV

What Are Models Like?

What sort of people are artist models? I once asked Boom Boom, and he said, "Crazy, demented, flamboyant, and exhibitionistic." I think he was projecting. Perhaps a common denominator was an interest in the visual arts and a willingness to be nude. Of course, for me, being part of a creation, getting lots of exercise, and being the star of my own show was a definite plus.

Models like the freedom and the variable hours involved, if not the pay. Some are dancers, musicians, artists, actors or writers. Most last about a year or two and then get depressed about having no money and move on. I lived on food stamps.

V

Where Did This All Start?

My family moved from a small town in New Jersey to Los Angeles when I was about to start junior high school in 1958. At that time, I had a thick New Jersey accent, my hair was weird and curly, and my clothes were not cool. I only had one friend. For the most part, if I wasn't being humiliated, I was at best shunned by most of the students.

One day, I was sitting in the auditorium when the school was putting on the play *The Diary of Anne Frank*. The idea that these students could be dressed up in costumes pretending they were someone else appealed greatly to me. I thought that perhaps I could hide behind a costume or a character and not have to face the daily torture of being unpopular. In high school, I signed up for drama, and it changed my life for the better. Not only was I accepted by this odd group of students, but it also seemed I had a bit of a talent. I decided that this was it for me. I was going to be an actress, period.

My fervor for acting continued, including four years majoring in theater arts at UCLA and another couple of years doing the

Hollywood, and the NYC scene. I unsuccessfully tried to get an agent for TV and/or movies in L.A. One of them actually told me to get my nose done and come back.

VI

Acting in New York City

Directions

I had a lot to learn about being an actress. Stuff you couldn't learn by being a student in a university. So, I just took a six month leave from UCLA and got on a plane to New York.

I thought that maybe I had to go to New York City and really experience what acting was all about and if I could really "make it." I had about $100 left after I bought the plane ticket. I thought that was a lot of money.

I had what I thought was a winter coat with me and had no idea where I was going to stay. I have a weird memory for numbers and remembered the address one of my pretentious fellow students had given me in case I ever wanted to visit her in New York City. Even though I had lived in New York and New Jersey as a child, I was now twenty years old and basically clueless about what it would mean to try to live in Manhattan.

I got there in July 1966. There was a heat wave, 104 every day for a week, 100% humidity, Hell. That woman's apartment building was air-conditioned in the lobby, and I miraculously found it. As I said, I have a weird memory for numbers. I'm not good at arithmetic, but I can remember numbers for some odd reason. I trudged in the heat with my suitcase to the address I remembered. And yes, her name was on the mailbox!

I waited in the lobby for her to come home. After taking me upstairs to her place that had large photographs of one of her housemates who was a *Vogue* model on the wall, she scarfed down several drugs, drank some wine, hopped in the shower, and then asked me if I wanted to join her.

Um, no. I would have loved to take a shower, but with her? At that time in my life, I didn't understand. I began to understand however when she said in her fake British accent, "I always thought you were different from other girls." *You did? And what does that mean? Ohhh, she's coming on to me!* That had never happened to me before, and I wasn't prepared for it.

She offered for me to sleep with her on her bed. I declined and slept on the couch. It took me quite a while to fall asleep, but once I realized she was zonked out, I did fall asleep. I left early in the morning, leaving my "winter coat" and went to the train station to stay with a family, close to where I used to live as a child in Maplewood, New Jersey.

They offered to let me stay as long as I needed until I found a place in New York. Luckily, I only stayed two nights.

The next day, I went over to NYU and tried unsuccessfully to use their housing board. "No, we won't give you any information. I don't care what the hell university you are going to," replied the student worker.

"Can I just sit here then? It's air-conditioned," I said.

"Well, okay. Knock yourself out."

After sitting there for about a half an hour and wondering what the hell I was going to do, a man came barreling into the room.

He was behind me, putting his hands on my shoulders and saying, "Do you need an apartment?"

Of course I answered, "Yes."

"Come with me" he said and I followed him to his VW bug.

Mind you I didn't know who he was. Here I was, 3,000 miles from home and getting into a strange man's car in the middle of NYC. In the car he told me that he was a professor in Brooklyn, he and his wife had separated and he bought a year's lease on an apartment. They were now back together, and he needed someone to sublease the last three months. He said it was fully furnished and was $150 a month. I told him I only had $100 to my name, which was unfortunately true. He nodded and said, "Let me talk to the landlady. We'll see what we can do."

He took me upstairs to what seemed to me to be a fantastic place. It wasn't air-conditioned, but, so what? I didn't know it was a block from what they called Needle Park at the time. 71st and Broadway.

The landlady agreed to let me stay there for $100 a month. I never found out if he paid the $50 or she just let it go. But, voila! I had an apartment on day 2 in NYC!

Of course, as I sat there drenched in sweat from the humidity, I thought, *Shit! I need to figure out how to pay for this!* The apartment had saltines and instant coffee in the cupboards. That was a good thing, because I had no money for food. It also had giant bugs called water bugs I was not too happy to find out.

When I went to take my first shower, one of these bugs was in the tub. I screamed, of course, and tried to find some Raid or something to kill it with. I couldn't find any insect killer, but I did find an old spray can of Aqua Net with which I used more than I probably needed on the poor thing. Then, I scooped it up with a cup, opened the window and tossed it out of the 6th story onto the patio below.

Luckily, there wasn't anyone walking around down there at the time. It would have been a rude awakening to get beaned by a shellacked water bug.

I slept in a wet towel that night during the heatwave. It worked well enough. The next day, I started to look for a job. *What the hell could I do?* I could type. I was horrible as a salesgirl, but I could do that, if needed.

As I was walking around in the heatwave, I saw a job agency. *Maybe it's air-conditioned?* I hoped so.

I told the guy about my measly job experience, which included typing for a company in Santa Monica that sold hair conditioners. There were four kinds, one of which looked like sperm, but really grew hair. I omitted that little detail. Then, I listened as he called a prospective job for me and said, "Yeah, I have here a lovely little lady from California who types 70 wpm on an electric typewriter...."

I waved my arms in protest. He waved me away.

"Why did you lie? I can't do that? I've never even seen an electric typewriter. And 70 words per minute?"

"You'll do fine. You have an interview tomorrow morning at 10:00 a.m. 500 Fifth Avenue. Business Film Association. Be there."

I didn't realize how prestigious it was until I got to the building. The Film Association was on the 6th floor. I walked in and a receptionist with a tight perm of slightly blue hair and long fingers looked me up and down as if I were an insect. I told her my name and she called someone on the switchboard to come from the back.

*   *   *

Suddenly, I was looking at a beautiful Puerto Rican woman with jet black hair, a gold cross, deep red lipstick, big gold earrings, a shocking pink suit, lovely brown skin, black high heels and I kid you not, a lit cigarette in a long black shiny cigarette holder.

"I'm Maria. Follow me. I'm going to give you a typing test,"

She turned and marched down a long corridor. I followed. She motioned for me to sit down in front of an electric typewriter.

"You're going to type scripts. That's the job. You can't make any mistakes. Mr. Parsons doesn't allow it. And don't think you can use Correcto-tape. If you do, Mr. Parsons will hold up the script to the light and rip it up in your face. Got it?"

She put down the script and some paper next to the typewriter. I looked at the typewriter, the front and the side. I didn't know how to put in the paper or how to turn it on.

"Um, I don't think we have this kind of typewriter in California."

Maria's eyebrows raised. She took a long drag off her cigarette.

"Oh yeah? Ok, sweetheart. I'll put in the paper for you and turn it on."

The typewriter made a humming noise.

"OK. You could start now. And remember, no mistakes."

She took another long drag off her cigarette. I leaned over and put my fingers on the keys. What? Suddenly there were several letters on the paper!

"I didn't mean to type those letters!"

I looked up at Maria.

"You're nervous, sweetheart. Start over."

I put my fingers on the keyboard again. Damn! It happened again! More letters were up there that made no sense. I slumped in my chair, tears welling up in my eyes.

"I'm sorry. He lied to you. They probably do have this kind of typewriter in California, only I've never seen one. I don't know how to type on an electric typewriter! I can type, but on a regular kind of typewriter. And 70 words a minute? I can maybe type 50. But no mistakes? Listen, I'm 3,000 miles away from home. I barely told my parents I was leaving. I don't know how I'm going to pay for this apartment now. I'm sorry."

Maria took another long drag off her cigarette and fingered her gold cross.

"Listen, sweetheart, we're going to be interviewing a lot of people for this job, but if we don't find anybody in three days, we'll give you a chance. I'm not making any promises, so don't get your hopes up. But, call me in three days."

*   *   *

I walked outside into the 104 degree heat, defeated. I walked past the New York City public library and thought they might have air conditioning in there, so I went inside. Ah yes. It was air conditioned. And there was a room off to the side that had electric typewriters in it with slots for quarters. You could type for 20 minutes for twenty five cents and they gave you the paper! I stayed there and practiced typing for 3 hours and went back again the next day. I used up $10.00. Considering I had about $15 left to last me until the end of the month or forever for all that I knew, that was a big deal. On day three, I went to a phone booth a block away from 500 Fifth Avenue and called Maria.

"Hi, Maria? I'm Helene Simkin. You know the girl from California? You will? Really? How soon? Well, I'm just a block away. I could be there in 5 minutes."

I earned $66.23 a week. To me that was a lot of money. I didn't eat much the first month though because I was afraid to. I basically lived on scrambled eggs and Oscar Meyer wieners. I'd stand over the stove, stab a wiener with a fork and cook it over the burner. Then I'd eat it standing up. I also found some instant coffee, Nestlé's, in the apartment which was fully furnished. I used that up fast.

One reason I loved my job was I got to clean up the staff lounge. Now, those of you who know me, know I don't like to clean much, but since I was starving, this was the ideal job for me. At 3:30 p.m.,

I went in there and after a brief and more than likely inefficient cleaning job, I helped myself to the saltines and hot chocolate mix in the cupboard above the sink. I didn't have time to make the hot chocolate, so I just emptied a packet into my mouth which was already stuffed with way too many saltines. Once, after I had stuffed my mouth, I saw, by looking in the mirror above the sink, August K. Capp, the Vice President of the company, open the door to the break room. Our eyes met and I began to choke uncontrollably. Saltines and hot chocolate powder spewed forth onto the mirror above the sink, while Mr. Capp kindly backed out, closed the door and left me to my coughing misery. He was such a nice man. He had that southern politeness.

I did have to type scripts. And perfectly. And yes, Mr. Parsons did rip up a script or two in my face when he saw that I had used Correcto-tape. For the first month or two, I would make a mistake and when I thought no one was looking, I'd stuff the paper into my purse. I stuffed many pieces into my purse. And, at the end of the day, I had the fattest purse in the elevator.

Another weird part of the job was helping Avis Sorgren, Mr. Parsons's secretary serve pastries and coffee to the clients who were viewing their films in the screening room. Invariably we would get our asses pinched and there was nothing we could do about it. Avis was a tall, beautiful Scandinavian-looking woman who wore mohair sweaters and tight pastel-colored skirts with her suede pumps. She had big blue eyes and ash blonde hair always perfectly done in an updo. The only thing amiss about Avis Sorgren were her fingernails. They were bitten to the quick. Once, I asked Avis how it was to work for Mr. Parsons.

"Well, he's very exacting, as you know. Every morning I have to serve him a Danish in the middle of the tray, with one cup of coffee to its left that has two sugars and one tablespoon of cream. There also has to be a tri-folded napkin just to the left of the plate as well. If it's not perfect, he yells and makes me do it over again."

"Oh."

Once in a while, Mr. Parsons would conduct an "office party." We would dutifully line up and walk into his vast office where folding chairs would be lined up against the walls. I'm sure Avis had to do that. Then we would sit cautiously in our chairs and wait to be offered Hawaiian Punch and cookies. After sitting back down, we would try to laugh at Mr. Parsons's jokes. I'm not sure who was more uncomfortable, Mr. Parsons or us.

A few weeks into my stay in the sweat lodge of the big Apple, I figured a walk through Central Park would be refreshing and beautiful. So, I set out, swinging my newly purchased burgundy handbag and my hips. The deciduous trees were gorgeous and the shade they provided was very much appreciated. And then I saw the pond. It wasn't very deep, and I was wiping the sweat off my brow, so I kicked off my sandals and started wading through the pond.

Then I noticed the man. He was leaning up against a tree with a notebook and a pen, staring at me. It looked like he was taking notes. He smiled. I returned the smile. He looked to be in his late twenties, wearing a nice looking pair of Dockers and a crisp powder blue button-down shirt.

"Excuse me. I couldn't help but notice how abandoned and happy you looked just now in the water with your shoes off."

"Yes, it feels so good. It's a warm day and that pond is so inviting."

Then, he continued to talk to me in a very unthreatening way.

"I hope you don't think this is too forward, but I'm a psychology student at NYU and I'm doing research. I'd like to interview you if I may."

I loved being interviewed.

"Sure, go right ahead," I said as I walked out of the pond and started to put my sandals back on.

He continued to smile at me.

"Oh, that's very kind of you. The thing is that some of the questions I need to ask you aren't appropriate for being outdoors. I was wondering", he said with a vaguely self-satisfied smile, "if you might know of someplace where we wouldn't be disturbed?"

I was the type of young woman who basically said yes to everything and then thought about the consequences later, after all, I had just hopped on a plane and traveled 3,000 miles away, so I blurted out, "Well, there's my apartment. It's only a few blocks from here."

He looked very pleased. "Oh, great! You wouldn't mind? I wouldn't want to impose. I mean, would your husband mind?"

"I'm not married."

"You're boyfriend?"

"I don't have a boyfriend."

"Your roommates?"

"I live alone."

Alarms should have gone off. They didn't.

As we entered my apartment, I was vaguely embarrassed that it wasn't all that clean.

He was standing against the wall in my living room with his pen in hand poised above his notebook.

He cleared his throat, saying, "So, I need you to take off your shoes for these series of questions."

Weird, but he is smiling reassuringly.

"Okay. I'd like to watch you walk across the hardwood floor in your bare feet slowly."

So, here's the deal. I was used to being directed as an actress. Being asked to walk across my floor barefoot seemed innocuous enough. Actually, kind of fun.

I thought maybe I should be a better hostess. "Want a glass of water?"

He shook his head. "Do you have any wine?"

"Um, no. Sorry. I have coffee."

"That's okay. I'm fine for now. Just walk across the floor for me."

I did and looked over at him to see if that was what he wanted. He was writing things down in his notebook.

"Was that okay?"

"Yes. That was great. Thank you. How did that feel?"

Huh? That was odd.

"Um, I don't know. Fine, I guess. "

"It didn't bother you to walk across the floor barefoot while I observed you and took notes?"

This guy is beginning to seem a bit weird. I mean, he asked me to do something, and I did it.

"No. Not really."

"That's what I like about you. You're so free. Where are you from if I might ask?"

"California."

"Oh. That explains it."

"It does?"

"Yes, from what I've heard, Californians are much less uptight than we on the East Coast are."

Well, maybe we are. Good for us.

"What class is this for?"

"What?"

"You said you were a psychology student. What class is this for?"

"Oh. Right. It's for Human Behavior."

Is he shitting me?

"Oh, okay."

"Ready for the next request?"

I guess so.

"Sure."

"I'd like you to walk across the floor and suddenly see a giant bug near your foot."

What the fuck?
"A bug?"
"A giant bug."
This guy is beginning to give me the creeps.
"And then what?"
"I just want to see what you'd do if you were walking barefoot and saw a giant bug on the floor near your feet."

Well, I've had had to do much stranger things in my acting classes. I'm not particularly afraid of bugs, but the idea of a giant one isn't too pleasant. Oh, what the hell.

He was still plastered to the wall with his pen and notebook. I did like the attention, although I was beginning to wonder just what I had gotten myself into. I started to walk across the floor.

"I want you to walk fast and not notice the bug until you've almost stepped on it. Don't look down."

What the hell is wrong with this weirdo?
"Don't look down?"
"No. Not right away."
Just fucking do it. He's giving you directions. Just do it.
"Okay."

I started walking and then looked down, lifting my foot to avoid the bug.

"Good," he nodded, smiling, and writing furiously in his notebook.

Of course, I was pleased that I had done a good job. I looked over at him expectantly.

He looked me directly in the eyes this time and said, "Now, I want you to squish the bug and kill it slowly with your bare foot."

Are you fucking kidding me?
"Squish it?"
"Yes."
"And kill it?"

"Yes."

I'd been asked to do many things in my classes before, but never anything this bizarre. Even if I tried Method acting skills, I couldn't imagine ever squishing a bug with my bare foot.

"I'm sorry", I said, feeling like I had let him down, "but I don't think I can do that."

His smile faded. "You have to."

What?

"I do?"

"Yes. It's for my assignment."

This is getting creepy.

"I'm sorry. I really am, but I don't think I can do that."

"Why not?" He looked almost angry. I didn't like disappointing him, but I was starting to wonder what might come next. I became aware of my heart beating erratically.

He was now gripping his notebook and pen and looking rather angry.

"You said you would help me."

My heart sank. I felt like I had failed a direction. *What kind of an actress was I if I couldn't do this?*

"I just can't. I would never squash a bug with my bare feet. I just can't imagine ever doing that."

"Why not?"

"Because it's creepy."

And then I saw the grin creep across his face, and felt as if someone had shaken me. I felt sick to my stomach.

"You. You need to leave now," I blurted out. I was shaking now.

"Leave?"

"Yes. Leave. You need to leave my apartment now."

We stared at each other. My knees felt weak.

Then, his body kind of collapsed as if he had been punched in the gut, looking dejected. I almost felt sorry for him.

Who the hell was he really? Why did I let him talk me into this?
My fear turned suddenly to fierce anger.

I yelled. "Get out now! Get the hell out of my apartment now or I'll call the police!" I practically spit those last words out, grinding my teeth and snarling my lip.

"Okay. Okay!" His hands shot up into the air as he turned towards the door, fumbling for the knob.

"Get out! Get out!" I screamed as he miraculously opened the door and fled down the steps of my brownhouse.

I ran to the door and double-locked it. Then I ran back to the window and watched as he fled down the street, my face flushed. I put my hand on my heart willing it to go back to normal.

He didn't do anything. He was just weird. He didn't do anything. He was just weird, I repeated.

I avoided going near that pond again as well as wading through ponds with my shoes off.

I'll never see him again, I hoped. And I didn't.

After a month or two they decided to send me to switchboard school so I could take over for Mrs. Gilda Steinmetz on her breaks. She wasn't very happy about this at all. I think she thought I wanted her job. Little did she know I'd rather stick needles in my eyes. She really hated me. She seemed suspicious that I was reading books like Clea, Balthazar and Justine while she was reading *Reader's Digest*. Before and after I took over for her at the switchboard, she would spray it all down with Lysol.

When I first took over the switchboard, she warned me in no uncertain terms.

"You know this switchboard has 15 lines and one red light. That red light is Mr. Parsons's. If you don't answer it by the third light, you will be fired immediately. And, you have to get the person he wants on phone before you call him back or he will fire you. Do you understand?"

I lived in fear of that red light.

One day Gilda Steinmetz was out ill. I had to take over for her all day long.

"Good morning, Business Film Association. Helene speaking. How may I direct your call?"

I said this all day long, trying not to look over at the red light of Mr. Parsons's that might possibly light up if I was very unlucky. Sure enough, at 3:30 p.m: blink, blink.

Oh my God! I had to answer it before the next blink!

"Yes, Mr. Parsons?"

"Get me the witch." Click.

The witch? The witch? Who was the witch? I grabbed the rolodex and looked under "W". Of course there was no "witch" there. I had to call him back even though I wasn't allowed to. *The witch. The witch.* It became like a mantra. Only unlike most mantras, it wasn't helpful at all.

"Um, Mr. Parsons? This is Helene. I know you know. I'm very sorry. I know I'm not supposed to call you back unless I have the person on the line, but I don't know who the witch is."

"My wife, God damn it." Click.

His wife? I looked under the "P's" and in Mrs. Steinmetz' constipated handwriting, I found "Mrs. Parsons."

"Hello, Mrs. Parsons? Your husband would like to speak with you."

"Oh yeah?"

I kept thinking the *witch, the witch* and guess what I didn't do? I didn't flip the toggle switch so that she couldn't hear.

"Mr. Parsons? I have the witch on the line."

There was a pause, and then,

"What did she say? The what?"

Oh no!!! I threw off the headphones. I was beside myself. *Oh my*

God! I'm going to be fired today. I'm going to be fired. I will no longer earn $66.23 a week. I'll have to give up my apartment. Oh my God!

At exactly 4 p.m. Mr. Parsons came through the door. I sat there with my head bowed, waiting for the words that would end my career. He walked past my desk not saying a word. As he got to the door, he stopped and turned around. I looked up as he tipped his hat to me and smiled.

"Thank you. I've been meaning to tell her that for years."

Mr. Parsons threw another office party when he knew I was leaving. He actually gave me a present. It was a snow globe with Central Park inside. Maria told me he had never given an employee a present before. I looked around the room at the people sitting in the folding chairs. Mrs. Gilda Steinmetz smiled at me for the first time. I didn't know she could smile.

As I walked out the door for the last time, the snow globe under my arm, I turned and saw Mr. Parsons standing in the reception area. He was almost never there except to come in and leave. Looking a little sheepish, he gave me a nod of his head and turned back to walk down the hall to his office.

*   *   *

I started auditioning for small roles on the weekends in off-off-Broadway shows. I got lucky and got a part in a traveling show of *Enter Laughing*. This was a show that actors who were out of work and just needed enough money for maybe coffee, could be part of. We got paid $7.00 per performance. A drunk actually walked onstage at one of the venues. That was fun. The coolest thing was that there were some actors who had been part of Second City, an improv troupe, and were temporarily out of work. They knew all the lines and could play parts interchangeably. Being onstage with them was such a joy. They were consummate professionals, they listened, they projected, they gave me something to work from.

Not all the acting experience I had in New York was great. I auditioned for what I presumed was a professional play and allowed a couple of rehearsals to take place in my apartment. To my surprise, when the director appeared, he was alone. When I questioned him about the other actors, he mumbled, "Oh, they'll be along next time." After I read a few lines for him (very inane script), it became obvious that he wasn't really interested in my acting ability, the play hadn't exactly gotten off the ground and he was a total bullshitter. He was in his fifties, more or less, had shoulder length hair and a beer gut. At one point, he turned to me with a sideways grin, a gold tooth glinting, and said, "I make women scream."

To which I did a double take and said, "What?"

"You heard me. I make women scream." At this announcement, I told him he had to leave and I was quitting the play. "Are you sure?" "Oh yes, I'm quite sure." He looked angry, storming to the door. He turned and faced me one last time, saying, "You can change your mind." "Get out!" was my reply. Years later, not only did I chalk that up to experience and luck that I didn't get raped, but I put that 'I make women scream' in a poem.

VII

Night on a Subway

Winter had settled in New York, with icy sidewalks and snow. I decided to treat myself and go to a Ravi Shankar concert.

This time I made the mistake of not doing my usual New York City single woman defense trick. I was so blissed out by the concert; I didn't put on the typical determined face and tough posture I usually did. It was around 2 a.m. Not a great time to be alone down in the subway station.

I looked around and wondered why no one else was there. It felt kind of creepy. However, the ragas were still dancing in my head. I had splurged on that concert because it was my last weekend in New York City. I'd been living 3,000 miles away from home for 6 months and I missed my little sisters a lot. New York was really a little too exciting for me. I don't think I ever had a good night's sleep. Not even once.

I began looking in the direction of where the train would come. And then I heard a sound. *Oh, what's that? I think I hear movement behind the pillar that's a couple of feet away.*

And then I saw it. A penis. I had not seen very many of them. I had barely given away my virginity a few months before I fled to New York.

I heard the train coming just as I saw a middle-aged, heavyset short man with bulging eyes appear from behind the column. The train's brakes screeched, the doors opened, and I bolted in. The man sat down directly across from me. My heart was beating off rhythm, my mouth parched, my head hot. The Ravi Shankar music was no longer in my memory, the concert forgotten.

He zipped up his fly and looked directly at me. There were a couple of people in the car, typical New Yorkers, minding their own business. I wished they wouldn't. I wished they could see how terrified I was.

I focused on the police officer patrolling our car. He looked young. I tried to catch his eye, my mind racing. He finally looked at me. And then I thought, *what am I going to say to him? How can I prove anything? Why would I know what a penis looks like? Will I have to stay longer in New York and miss my flight home if I had to testify or anything?* I looked away and held my breath.

At my stop as the doors opened, I scrambled off the car and started climbing the 20 or so stairs to the street level. I could hear the man running behind me, grunting, huffing, yelling, "Pussy! Whore! Slut!"

The brownstone I was living in was two blocks away. I wanted to run, but my legs suddenly turned to cement walking in quicksand. I couldn't run. What was wrong with my legs? I was still a little bit faster than he was, but only ahead by a few feet. As I approached my building, I reached into my purse for my keys. I could hear him continue to grunt, pant and yell, "Pussy! Whore! Slut!" *Oh God, he was gaining on me.* I finally found the right key for the front door of the building, turned it, opened it and ran down the hallway. I searched frantically for the remaining three keys I needed to get into my apartment.

I could tell by how dark it was that my roommate wasn't home. She was hardly ever home, too busy picking up married men in bars. One – click – two – click – three- clicks. I was inside, slamming the door shut, just as he fell against it with a thud.

He pounded on the door as I was locking it from the inside. I collapsed onto the floor, next to the door, ready to keep it closed with my weight if need be. He pounded and yelled for what seemed like an eternity. And then it stopped. I put my ear next to the door hearing him walk down the hallway muttering to himself, cursing me.

I waited until I heard the front door of the building shut before I curled up into a fetal position on the floor. Several hours later, maybe 4 a.m., I heard a gentle knock.

I jumped up, peeked out the keyhole and saw a young man of about 25 standing there asking for Monica, my roommate. I responded through the closed door that she wasn't home. He then asked if he could come in. I hesitated but opened the door a crack. Looking at me, he said, "What's wrong? Did something happen?" I started to tremble as he opened the door and took me in his arms. He held me for what seemed like close to half an hour, patting my back and saying, "Poor baby. It'll be all right. You're okay now. You're safe." We spent the next few hours before the sunrise in my front room on the couch, sitting side by side. He held my hand. When we saw the first pink of the sky from my window, he told me he was going to insist that we go outside, get a coffee and go into the subway. He said he wanted my last experience in New York City to be a good one and to ride the subway feeling safe.

I will never forget that angel. I never even got his name.

VIII

Pathway from Theater to Artist Model

One of my childhood idols was Roberta Ostroff, the older sister of my best friend from junior high. Roberta had already graduated high school and did bitchin' things, like sleep naked on a mattress on the floor with a poster of Lenny Bruce on the wall. She looked sexy, smoking cigarettes, and spoke in an enticing, low, raspy voice. And she was a writer; I was very impressed with that. She wrote porn, though at that time I didn't really know what that meant. But I believed her when she said it ruined her sex life, because she said what she wrote was way better than what was happening in her real life.

Roberta always made everyone feel at home. She was a good listener. Once, I was talking to her on the phone, and I heard the toilet flush. I asked her about it, and when she admitted to being on the toilet, I was shocked. How could she concentrate on two things at once?

I think one reason she made me feel so comfortable was that she always continued to do whatever she was doing almost as if you weren't there at all. She'd talk on the phone, put on makeup, type or whatever. She always had a typewriter with paper in it, an ashtray, a cup of coffee, a makeup mirror, tweezers, mascara, lipsticks, nail polish and remover and face creams. She looked like she was about to get up from whatever she was doing. She told me she had been fat in high school, and because of that she never wanted to appear as if she was going to eat. She used words like "tough," "bitchin'," "groovy," "boss." She rolled these words around in her mouth and then coyly spit them out at whomever she was talking to. I wanted to be her.

During the time I was in L.A., trying to be an actor, I would visit my parents in Big Sur, California. In the late 1960s my father, Jim Simkin, who was a Gestalt therapist, held his own workshops and worked alongside Fritz Perls at Esalen Institute. It is a Big Sur retreat center that was called an "intentional community".

Fritz Perls was often at our house. My dad was his protégé. He once told me I would never amount to anything but a housewife, and he bought me a frying pan for Hannukah. *Thanks, asshole.* He would ask me for recommendations of good movies though. On another occasion, when I told him I had a one-line part in a play at UCLA, he told me he was a brilliant director and told me how to say my one line. I did it his way the next day. They cut that line.

Esalen played a key role in the Human Potential Movement beginning in the 1960s. Situated in Big Sur on a bluff overlooking the Pacific, it is known for its mineral baths, organic farm-to-table food and a variety of workshops on subjects like Tai Chi, yoga, dance and various modes of therapy.

Eventually, my dad had a falling out with Esalen. He called it "Poison Ville". His objection was that he felt they hired people who were unqualified to give workshops, were only in it for the money and were subjecting people to possibly dangerous outcomes. Somehow, our dog, Squareface, an Irish Setter, must have picked up on my dad's attitude because he once bit one of Esalen's co-founders Dick Price, on the butt as he jogged on highway 1 past our property. Both my dad and Dick got a good laugh out of that incident.

Another time, while visiting my father, I stood in the line for dinner at Esalen when someone asked me how old I was. (I later found out it had been actress Dyan Cannon, and that possibly she had joined the many others who were tripping on acid.) Her eyes appeared unfocused, but then, so were mine. When I responded "sixteen," she sighed and said, "How refreshing." Looking at me again, she asked me what I was into. I said I was an actress.

"Oh, you'll get over that. You really can't know what you'll be doing in five or ten years."

I was highly insulted. To my young mind, of course, I would always be an actress. This was my talent, my escape, my art. By that time, I had dedicated seven years of my life to it.

IX

Improv Troupe in Silverlake

In 1969, or so, I was working with an improvisational theatre group in Silverlake, near Los Angeles. I was new to the troupe. There was an unpleasant woman in her 40s, thin, with dark brown hair, who seemed to be the director. Another member of the troupe was a hirsute, 6'4" guy from Holland named Jake. And then, there was Norbert from Germany. He was a lyrical soul, slight of build, and had his light blond hair pulled back into a ponytail. There was a young woman about my age (22 or so) named Patty, who was famous for making sure her beautifully round behind was bare during performances.

Jake told us one night that he and his current girlfriend were making passionate, noisy love in their upstairs apartment when they heard a group of people in the street clapping. They both looked out the window, naked, smiling and took a bow.

The way the group worked was that we would rehearse on Mondays, Tuesdays and Wednesdays after first doing yoga, which was led by that unpleasant woman with the dark hair. The actors deferred to her. Then, on Thursdays we would all go to a therapist and "work out issues" that might have arisen during rehearsals. At the end of the therapy session, we were all expected to hug each other. We performed for audiences on Fridays, Saturdays and Sundays.

There are a few situations I remember very clearly. The way our troupe was set up was that we would trade off being the lighting person, the musician (a box of instruments, like maracas, drums, etc.) and the set "designer". Those sets consisted of black wooden boxes which we could easily move around. The rest of us would be the "actors" for that particular scene. We were to go backstage, look through boxes of costumes and props, choose whatever, if anything, we wanted to use, not talk to each other and get ready to enter. When the person who was in charge of sets had placed them on the stage, the person in charge of the lights would get ready, and the person who was going to do the music would go choose an instrument or noisemaker of some sort and sit down. Then, the actors, upon hearing the music and seeing the lights, would enter onto the set they had never seen before, perhaps wearing a new costume for the first time or—as was the fashion in the late '60s—wear nothing at all. Jake, the guy from Holland, was very fond of being buck naked. His black curly hair were a prominent feature all over his body.

One of the three most memorable times was when I was onstage with Norbert, the German. Backstage, I had grabbed a globe, and onstage, after it had worked its way into being my womb in the scene, I gave birth to the world. It was quite pleasant, and Norbert and I were a loving couple.

Another time was on Halloween. Jake had stripped and was handcuffed to a folding chair for a scene. However, when the scene terminated, no one could find the key to the handcuffs, so he had to crawl off stage attached to the chair and go into the green room. At the end of the evening, they all appointed me to call the cops to try and get the handcuffs off. I suppose they appointed me because I was the youngest and most innocent looking. I called, and the response was, "All right, we'll come out, as long as you don't call us pigs." So, we begged Jake to at least allow us to put underwear on him.

Norbert had put on a grey flowing costume that looked like a sheet and painted on a skeleton face. He refused to take off any of his costume and placed himself at the piano, which was against the wall in the foyer, several feet away from the door to the theatre. When the cops came in, Norbert started playing the piano to the beat of how the cops walked. He had the sheet music for Rachmaninoff's *Concerto No. 2*. One of the cops was very nervous and dropped his billy club. Of course, that fit in quite nicely to the music Norbert was banging on the old, funky upright.

I then quickly steered the cops into the theatre where Jake was sitting handcuffed to a folding chair in his underwear. He seemed more disgruntled at being made to wear underwear, than at being handcuffed to the chair. The cops looked sideways at each other, and the taller one with the kinder face took out the keys. They tried, unsuccessfully, for about five minutes, and then after commiserating with each other, told us that *these* particular handcuffs were Japanese. They only had keys for American handcuffs. At this, trying to maintain a professional demeanor, they left. Of course, Norbert was still at the piano and accompanied their exit with Tchaikovsky's *Romeo and Juliet*.

What were we going to do? The three of us who had cars, for some bizarre reason, had Volkswagen (VW) Bugs—not conducive to transporting a tall, mostly naked guy handcuffed to a folding chair. We took out the passenger seat of one of the Bugs and folded 6'4" Jake into the car. Patty knew someone with an electric saw in their garage, and they had agreed to try and saw off the handcuffs. Three hours later, Jake was folding-chair and handcuff free. Trick or treat?

The last incident I remember was when I was barefoot onstage during a scene with the older woman, who I had suspected didn't like me. She proceeded to break a Coke bottle near my feet, so I was unable to move. Hostile environment? I think so.

At the Thursday therapy session, I confronted her. I was seething. She feigned innocence. Understanding that she was basically in charge of this troupe, I said, "Okay. What you did was inappropriate and threatening. Since you call the shots with this troupe, I'm out." I opened the door and never returned.

Before I had left the troupe, the man next door to where we rehearsed came up to me one day and asked if I would be his model for the evening. He had an art class of some kind which paid his rent, and his model wasn't going to show. He seemed like an okay guy. He had a ponytail, wore a T-shirt and jeans with beat-up white sneakers.

I didn't know what to say. I had never done anything like *that* before. The whole idea made me nervous. He pleaded with me, worked on my guilt about his rent (guilt usually works on me), and told me he'd pay ten dollars for three hours. I had gotten a ten-dollar parking ticket that morning. I soon agreed, as long as he'd show me what to do before the class. I figured I could use it as an acting experience, and also, I could take my glasses off, so I wouldn't be able to see anyone's reaction. The nudity part didn't bother me, as I weighed the least I'd weighed since I was 15 and was actually proud of my body for the first time in seven years. It was the idea of doing a bad job that bothered me.

The man then proceeded to show me "how to model." He sat in a chair and thrust out his chest coquettishly. Then, he spread his legs apart and gave me a "come hither" look. I was reminded of the photos I'd seen in my boyfriend's Playboy magazines. He did more cheesecake poses as I stared at him. I couldn't believe it. I made up my mind then to do whatever came into my head and forget his ideas. He suggested that I take off my clothes before the class got there, so I wouldn't be embarrassed, and gave me a robe to wear.

That night was the beginning of a new life for me. I have probably never worked harder as a model than I did that night, because I didn't know what my body could hold as a pose and for how long. I braved it, my body shaking while I held my arms above my head for ten minutes like an idiot. I was sweating and didn't dare talk to anyone. At the end of class, I looked at the drawings one by one, silently walking by and peeking over people's shoulders. Wow! I was impressed. So were they. As I looked at someone's drawing, I would get comments like, "You're the best model we've had in a long time" and "Oh, you must model for my other class. You're fantastic!" and "Where can I reach you to work for me?" That was certainly positive. Very positive. Just about the opposite experience from Hollywood. Also, these artists felt sincere. There was no undercurrent of competition in the room— another reaction I wasn't used to as an actress.

Years later, when I had decided to write this book, I was telling a fellow-model friend about it, when she said that she thought *you either have it or you don't* as a model. She was very sure of this and was trying to convince me. I don't believe this altogether. I think you can learn to be a good model. You don't even need to be that self-confident. I certainly wasn't. I may have been proud of my body, but I was very insecure about my ability to model. What happened for me was a gradual self-confidence in a new art form. This led to my having a lot more faith in myself. I learned to love and appreciate myself like never before. Instead of being in a field where rejection was the name of the game, as an artist model I was the star of my own show. When I saw a drawing that I felt captured the feel of what I was trying to get across, it was very exciting. I felt that the artist and I had communicated non-verbally. This was quite spiritual for me. I suppose that's the meaning of the word "art" for me. I felt quite content in those days.

I soon began to realize this artist model trip was far better than anything I'd ever been into. I didn't get asked to get my nose done and come back, lose weight or straighten my hair. I was actually appreciated more for being myself in whatever form I came in and I could be very creative with my body movements. There were 30-second, 5-, 10-, and 20-minute poses. If I had to do the same pose for the whole class period, I could do it in 20-minute segments and take breaks. I could set a mood with my poses, get exercise, acceptance, and immediate gratification. I was part of something artistic. I didn't feel that I was working. I was getting paid for having fun. It was love at first sight for me and modeling, which was the way I used to feel about acting. I thought I would never stop and felt totally dedicated. Of course, now I know Dyan Cannon was right. One can never really know what they will be doing in five years.

X

Modeling in Southern California and Los Angeles

It was 1970, and I had started worked for a lot of painting classes at UCLA, LA City College, Otis Art Institute, and Santa Monica City College. After that, there were other schools and—the most fun—private groups.

In the beginning, I found out about a booking agent for models and worked for him. He got 10%. He was also a prick. He would call at 7:00 a.m. and send me out on a job about an hour or so away. In other words, whoever worked for him got all the lousy jobs. I found out soon enough that only the mediocre models, the ones who didn't know any better or how to hustle jobs on their own, worked for him. I found out that all I had to do was walk up to a life-drawing teacher, introduce myself as a model, tell them I needed work, and usually got a booking right there and then. I have discovered that most teachers never have the heart to turn down anyone at any time who wants to model for them. It usually only took asking the teacher once. Art teachers don't like to be bothered with lots of details, like setting up models for their classes. It's a lot easier for them to say to whomever is there at the moment, "Can you come next week, too?"

The good thing about private drawing groups is that they usually met in a nice home, with good heating and lots of big cushy pillows. I'd walk up to homes that had vast lawns and beautifully manicured shrubbery, to knock on elaborate thick doors that on occasion even had stained glass windows. Inside, there were paintings on the walls, sculptures placed strategically in immaculate and tasteful rooms. There was a sense of warmth, safety, and luxury. It was a far cry from some of the classrooms in the broken-down buildings in downtown Los Angeles, where the heaters were few and far between and various people, not associated with the art class, could wander in unannounced at any given time. Also, they weren't watching every goddam second you took a break. They served tea and cookies, sometimes wine. Everyone was in a hang-loose mood. They often had Brahms or Chopin piped in, to help set the scene.

L.A. was traditional. In my experience, many of the teachers, though luckily not all of them, wanted classical poses, like in the paintings and sculptures from the 19th century. I always was asked to take off my glasses, which cut me off from the world. I had to resort to a lot of fantasy. While that was definitely enjoyable, I preferred contact with the artists. When I did get to wear my glasses, I would study the people in the room, their postures, everything about them, just like I had done for my acting classes in the past.

Grecian Vase Pose
Anonymous

While many of the teachers preferred the classical poses, some of the teachers in Los Angeles were pretty inventive. They would get off on making up an unusual setup, and I would arrive only to melt into a fantastic little scene. Once there was a sailboat in the classroom. Other times, there would be levels and varied patterns of cloth or styrofoam materials and wooden structures, where I would climb to the top and become part of the design. So, in a sense, the teacher and I would work together to create a scene that would give the students inspiration. Because it took so long getting into or onto the structure, this usually happened in painting classes. In drawing classes, one did anywhere from 30-second to 20-minute poses, and if a model had to try and extract her/himself from a complicated structure after each pose, it would have been difficult and wasted a lot of time.

Painting classes had another bonus: silence. I suppose, because the artists had to concentrate on one long pose for up to three hours, they were less apt to chitchat.

All I could hear were paintbrushes on canvas. The teacher would walk by and quietly discuss each student's work, while I watched. I was aware of every little movement. The students soon forgot that I was anything more than a part of the scene up on the stand. Artists tended to forget after a while that I had eyes and ears and was alive. I sometimes felt as if I were watching an Andy Warhol movie, like *Sleep*—although it was a lot shorter than five hours and 20 minutes, and hopefully a lot less boring.

The fact that people forgot that I was actually a living, breathing body gave me unexpected voyeuristic opportunities. I felt like a nude "Peeping Tom", or should it be "Peeping Tomasina". One time, in a school in L.A., I was doing a 20-minute pose and there was a couple making out right in front of me. The guy was in his twenties, had long, dirty blond hair cascading to his shoulders. He was slight of build with a thin mustache and long, bony fingers. The young woman who sat next to him (or rather, almost on top of him) had curly auburn hair, a ski-jump nose and startling blue eyes, and was bursting out of her tight, hot-pink tank top and jeans. She got up and left the room momentarily as another young woman came in, sat in her seat and proceeded to make out with the guy as well. The second woman was Nordic-looking with blonde hair, high cheekbones and silver-grey eyes. Her cleavage was the most prominent feature. After several hot kisses and gropes, the door opened, and Woman #1 spied Woman #2, stormed in, grabbed her books and drawing paper, gave a few memorable glares at the two of them, and fled.

The guy, amusingly enough, didn't seem to be aware of Woman #1 at all. He was just enjoying the present moment, as it were. The song *Love the One You're With* kept echoing in my head. My pose was then over. The next time I was facing that direction, the Woman #2 had also left.

While I was enjoying modeling's voyeuristic opportunities, I was also getting an art education. I was learning about famous artists and instruction about drawing, painting and sculpture, perspective, negative space, light and dark. This was a definite bonus.

Modeling did a lot for my ego. When I was actively into being an actress in Hollywood, I thought I was supposed to look like everyone else. I managed a poor imitation of Marlo Thomas, straightening my hair every three months for $25 a pop. My hair looked like straw, but it was straight. My idol at the time was Shelley Winters. I thought that she epitomized what I was hoping to become: a competent and well-liked actress.

One day, I told a wonderful teacher named Jean Barlow, that I actually had frizzy hair. She made me promise that the next time I worked for her I would wear my hair like that. I was terrified, but I did it. This was in the late '60s, early '70s, when the hippie generation was just beginning to get underway. When I showed up to class with my hair naturally curly, the students loved it. My life changed in a big way after that. I fell in love with modeling. Here was a job that allowed me to be creative and reinforced my natural state of being. The truer to my nature I was, the more I was appreciated. This was a far cry from what agents were telling me. The people who thought I had "let myself go," when I allowed myself to be more natural, soon became less important to me, except my father. I was very sad that he didn't like it when I wore my hair naturally.

I embraced modeling and pretty much divorced myself from the Hollywood scene, where it seemed important to be seen at certain places with certain people, act certain ways, look certain ways, etc. That life was demeaning and exhausting. It had little to do with talent, but more to do with who you knew or whose son or daughter you were. You were always second-guessing what people wanted from you.

Musing
Claire Dolan, '78

XI

Santa Monica

During the first year that I modeled, I worked for a man named John in a warehouse in Santa Monica. Several other people were sharing that same space. One day, I was introduced to one of the other occupants. He was a very handsome man with a big, grey beard and long, grey hair. He looked like a mountain man. He said he worked with wood and did sculptures and that he was looking for a model. I consented to work for him in his studio; that was also his home.

It was soon evident that he couldn't draw worth beans. He kept apologizing for his drawings, saying he hadn't drawn in a year. I began to detect a faint glimmer of hope, to the effect that he had ulterior motives in asking me to work for him. I was casually reading some bullshit astrology book and smoking a joint with him, when I chanced upon the section on Virgos (he had told me that was his sign). It said they were lousy lovers. I laughed out loud (meanwhile, creaming in my jeans). He asked me what was so funny. I told him. He then proceeded to show me that it wasn't true, at least, not in his case. It turned out that he was dating a Zsa Zsa Gabor-type jealous woman, and he was very uptight, thinking she might find out that I had been with him, especially in the morning. I said, "That's simple. I'll leave." He was amazed that I was so agreeable. It was all the same to me.

Soon after that I went into hiding. I told all involved that I was going nuts and needed to be alone. John was the only one who bothered to call me a few weeks later and tell me that whenever I came out of my hibernation, he was available, and he cared. The word "cared" worked wonders. I soaked that up.

Apparently, Zsa Zsa was no longer in the picture. We soon embarked on a six-month affair. He was almost twice my age, looking like he could have been my father. I remember the first time I woke up in bed next to him and looked at his wrinkled and ropey hand. I kind of freaked out a bit, but he wasn't old in any other way.

John did the coloring for Disney children's books. In his little office, he had drawings of all these little Disney characters on the wall and on his desk. He was an incredible craftsman. During the time we were together, he entered a contest that a department store was having, in which one had to design a light fixture. The first prize was $2,000. That was a lot of money in those days. He constructed a fantastic light in the shape of a huge lightbulb cut in half, so it could be hung on the wall. The night before he was going to present it, he dropped it and it broke into pieces on the floor. I watched as he dropped to his knees and cried. We went out in the middle of the night, got some glue and spent hours putting it back together a la Humpty Dumpty. He won!

The sad thing was that he was the kind of person who was afraid of success and never finished making the design for the department store to copy. One thing that was beginning to turn me off about him was that he would drink a lot of wine at night and space out to the point that one of his eyes was facing the wall, the other looking straight ahead. When he was drinking, he was unapproachable. He also had a habit of driving spaced out and crossing over the lines on the street telling jokes or stories to the people in the back seat.

We went on a trip to Arizona together with his wonderful, female German Shepherd named Jerry. I think this trip was the beginning of the end for us. A lot of it had to do with my knuckles being constantly white from his erratic driving.

I was in love with his dog, however. She was affectionate and sweet. I felt that John ignored her. Her eyesight wasn't too good. One of the things she would do is sneak up on objects in the street, like tires. This would embarrass John, but delight the people who would stare at her, amused. When we split up, I cried a lot. Not about John, but about Jerry. I was looking for a person a little more present.

One night before we broke up, a friend of John's, Louis, came over to show some slides or something. Talk about opposites. Louis was like an energy flash. He seemed more than alive, if that was possible. Soon enough, I developed a crush on him, variety being the spice and all. I soon began seeing Louis. John and Louis had a few little talks. The truth was that I was finished with John, and if it hadn't been Louis, it would have been someone else.

John, by the way, was almost never without a girlfriend. It wasn't long before he was in the middle of another torrid affair. John moved somewhere north of San Francisco to the mountains. I heard he built his own house, grew his hair down to his ass, and I'm sure, attracted every woman who passed by. He drove down to Disney Studios, every once in a while, for a freelance coloring job and then retreated to his abode in the woods. At the time of this writing, I don't know if he still lives there or if he's even alive. Louis sadly died of AIDS years ago. I found this out at a funeral for Eduardo Carrillo, a dear friend of ours who was also a painter.

Louis and I lasted about six months. He was a unique man. He never had a bad word to say about anyone, ever. To Louis, everything was *great*. He was always going to a *great* movie or to a *great* opening, or a *great* restaurant or a *great* party. The thing was he was always on his way to something. I couldn't keep up with him. He was also a good cook. His Sicilian relatives taught him how to make A+ spaghetti and omelets with loads of garlic. He loved to throw parties, where he invited people to dress up in costumes, as he loved to do that himself. He was very theatrical.

He had a big shower in his house in which we'd play games. In the shower, my name was Louise. We pretended that we didn't know each other but had just met in the shower. It usually started with, "Haven't I met you somewhere before?"

He was a generous man. He'd let anyone stay at his house for an indeterminate amount of time, if they needed to. He also loved children and had infinite patience with them. They could do or say just about anything and he wouldn't get mad. However, if he ever did get mad, that was not a good thing. I might add here that he was not only part Sicilian, but part Irish as well. He was small, muscular and dark. He had large, dark eyes that darted here and there with unabashed excitement; one of his nicknames was Louis the Dart Lunetta.

He and his first wife had lived in Ghana for a year or two. They had two beautiful children there born to the beat of African drums. In his house in Los Angeles, he had many sculptures and masks from Africa. He paid homage to the flora of Africa by his paintings in the house. In his front yard he had an enormous aviary and bamboo garden. The great thing about his eccentricity to me was that people looked at him, not me for a change. He would often wear colorful billowing pants, tight undershirts that showed off his muscled arms and shoes that curled up at the ends. I heard in later years that he had been in a Tai Chi commercial.

One night he decided to invite my father to dinner. This was a big deal. I warned Louis that my father was very critical of the men I chose, but Louis was not intimidated by anyone. He was looking forward to meeting him. He made a fabulous fish meal, and we seemed to be having a pretty good time. Soon after that night I asked my father what he thought of Louis. His response? "He's effeminate and he mumbles." I told Louis what he said, and he laughed. My dad also didn't like his looks, which was amusing to me because they slightly resembled each other.

XII

Modeling with Someone Else

One of the nicest experiences in modeling is when you get to model with another person. It's a different way of posing, relating to another person's body and their pose. You can feel them breathing, sweating, sometimes burping and, occasionally, farting. Sometimes, it's the first time you've met that person. It's like silent improvisational dancing, except nude. Sometimes, it becomes quietly talkative. It's so much fun. Unlike me, some models hated posing with someone else. Those models don't like to share the stand, as it were. They have to be the star of the show. When I worked with someone else (usually a gay guy, but not always), the conversation between the two of us became rather smutty. We could see the artists who were the closest to us, straining their little ears to hear every juicy tidbit that we were talking about. This behavior, of course, encouraged us to become even smuttier.

The first time I ever modelled with someone else is worth

mentioning. In the first place, I had no idea that I was going to work with another model, and I had very little experience. I walked into the classroom and there was a guy in a robe. I thought, *he's probably more comfortable drawing in a robe*, never imagining that we would be working together. I walked up to him and smiled. He looked at me, grinning.

"Oh, I guess we're working together," he said.

Working Together
Anonymous

My eyes got *really* big. I tried to appear smooth and sure of myself. Luckily for me, he had been modeling for quite some time and directed the whole thing. It worked out well. He turned out to be a rather strange person. He was about 38 years old, had an incredible tan, looked like he lifted weights every hour and brushed his teeth often. He belonged to a nudist camp in Palm Springs and invited me to come with him some day. I took him up on it.

I wasn't about to go alone, however, so I invited Patti, my girlfriend and fellow model, to come with me. I don't remember why, but an economics professor also came along. I think Patti invited him.

This had to go down as one of the weirdest double dates of my life. It took us a long time to get there, in my buff, male model friend's 1969 VW Bug. I tried to make small talk, but he seemed incapable of normal conversation. All he would talk about was health foods and lifting weights.

After about two excruciatingly uncomfortable hours crammed into the VW Bug, we got to the parking lot of the nudist camp. We were instructed to disrobe there but to leave our tennis shoes on. This was because the pavement was so hot. So, here we were in the middle of the desert, clad only in tennis shoes. The owners of the camp came out to the parking lot to greet us. The husband looked like a tan, well-preserved Elvis with a giant cross hanging around his neck. He had grey hair and one eye that was facing the east, while the other looked straight ahead. Of course, he had on tennis shoes. His wife, whose name was Ginger or Cookie, had dyed red hair, done up in a French twist, Pepto Bismol-colored plastic earrings and similarly colored baubles around her neck. She had on a ton of makeup. To go with that, she had gold lamé, open-toed, high-heeled shoes with scarlet-painted toenails and matching fingernails. I couldn't help but notice her enormous breasts with a plethora of freckles on her very tan body. The husband-and-wife team looked at us with patronizing smiles. They only looked at our faces, as if to reassure us that they wouldn't stare at our nude bodies. I, however, was staring at theirs.

Inside the camp, there was one little building that housed toilets and a Coke machine, a few nudist colony magazines and "that's all folks." Outside, there was a swimming pool, a badminton court without a net, and a patio where there were about seven portly, over-fifty nude Germans talking in German about who knows what. They were also wearing tennis shoes.

Aside from that, there were hills of cacti and open arid fields. It was very cloudy.

The four of us already knew we had nothing much to say to each other, Patty and I exchanging occasional glances as if to say, "Is this really happening?" At one point, without my glasses on, I decided to take a shower. I walked right past the Germans, who stopped talking to stare at me. Walking up to the pole that I assumed to be a shower, I tried to turn it on unsuccessfully three times. I felt around for something to push or pull to no avail. The Germans were still looking at me as I realized that this was not indeed a shower, but a light on a pole over the pool. I looked over their way, not being able to see them exactly because my glasses were off, and made a half-hearted attempt at laughing at my silly mistake. I then walked over to the cement slab I had been lying on before, pretending that nothing ridiculous had just happened.

Mr. Bodybuilder, white teeth, tan artist model, Patty, Mr. Economics Professor and I decided to take a hike. I'm sure we hiked pretty carefully that day, considering we only had on tennis shoes and were walking mainly amidst various cacti. When we returned, we made an attempt to bask in the fog for a little while longer. I felt sorry for the poor economics professor, who, due to his embarrassment at being naked, had lain on his stomach trying to hide his hard-on. Consequently, he left the camp looking like a lobster from the back. I refrained from looking at the front.

Driving back to L.A., we ate some health-food sesame crackers – talking, yet again, about nothing. As I looked out the car window, watching the desert turn slowly into the city, I felt a sigh of relief.

XIII

Glad to See a Cop

People used to ask me if modeling was ever scary. Not usually–but one time does come to mind. I was working for a class in downtown Los Angeles. There was a very good-looking guy in the class. He looked like he spent hours in the gym. He also had tattoos on his neck and shoulders. It was kind of hard to read the expression on his face. He looked like he had a few stories to tell. We started talking on my breaks and agreed to get together sometime in the near future.

The next time I worked for the class, he was there, except this time he seemed changed. He looked very stoned. It didn't seem like marijuana. He could hardly keep his eyes open. I told him the deal was off about getting together. When I told him that, his eyes turned to ice. He informed me he had just gotten out of Soledad Prison, and nobody told him, "No." I held my breath.

At the end of class, I stalled around, as long as I could, and told the instructor, Charlie White, what had happened. He offered to walk me to my car in the parking lot. We looked around and it seemed safe enough for Charlie to go back into the classroom.

I got in my red '66 VW Bug and began to turn out of the parking lot onto the street. I heard another car start up. Realizing who it was, I was afraid for my life. I tried to lose him in traffic, but he followed close behind me. Then, like in a cops-and-robbers movie, I made a few quick maneuvers while trying to find the nearest police station. Looking in my rearview mirror, I saw police lights flashing. Boy, was I relieved!

I stopped my car in the middle of the street, opened my car door and ran straight towards the police car. I stopped dead in my tracks, however, when I saw the cop pull his billy club out and raise it over my head. I froze, looked into his scared eyes and tried to talk, but couldn't.

Luckily, he had a partner who was a little more willing to hear my side of the story without bashing my brains out. I finally managed to stutter out the story about the guy chasing me, while the first cop was telling me in his authoritative voice that I had made an illegal left turn, or some other bullshit. For a minute, I thought he was actually going to give me a ticket.

The other cop was listening to me and looked concerned (I wondered if he was new). The first cop kept repeating the address of the nearest police station and reminded me several times of the traffic violations I had committed. He then told me I could be on my way.

In a daze, I drove to my sweetie's home, sure the guy would be waiting for me at some stoplight along the way. I never modelled for that school again. I heard from Charlie, later, that that guy never returned either.

When I modelled for Charlie, I didn't know he was a famous, African-American artist. To me, he was just one of the coolest teachers I had worked for. He was also a terrific flirt and a great person. When I'd model for his class, he'd be in the back of the classroom listening to Coltrane on the radio and dancing. He was real loose. I used to sit up there and watch him dance by himself. He had a good old time in the back of the class. His way of teaching was personable, human, and full of compassion. He was never uptight. Always warm. He was probably about 60 years old then. He had a big Afro, white hair, a slight pot belly, and a whole lot of style.

XIV

Racism

One time in L.A., a man called me up and asked me to model for a group downtown. It was a small group of older men who had been drawing together for years. He asked me to get a male model to pose with, but he said the model couldn't be black. I asked him why. He mumbled something unintelligible. So, when I hung up, I immediately called the only black male model I knew and told him the story. He agreed to do the job with me. I suppose this was spiteful on both our parts, but so fucking what. Like me, Van, who happened to be the best model in L.A. at the time (at least in my opinion), wanted to prove a point to these racist bastards. Unfortunately, we were the ones learning the lesson. Van showed up before I did. He told me the conversation went a bit like this:

Older man (shocked): Yes?
Van: Hi! I'm one of your models for tonight.
Older man: Oh... I see.
Van: May I come in?
Older man: Yes...uh, what does Helene look like again?

Van: Well, (smiling) she's short, and round, and has frizzy hair.

Older man: (hoping for more of a racial description) Oh? Frizzy hair?

Van: (knowing what he wants to know and not telling him) Yes.

Then I appeared on the scene and saw the shock registering on the faces of all the older white men who were sitting in front of their easels. Van and I decided to have a good time, no matter what the vibrations were in the room. We took lots of elegant, classically romantic poses. During our breaks we were laughing and having a good old time. At the end of the evening, we decided to have a look at their drawings. The majority of them had drawn me crying or frightened and Van without a face. One of them changed the pose somewhat to look like he was raping me. I was stunned. Van looked resigned. We looked into their faces, knowing it was the artist's prerogative to see things any way they wanted to, to leave things out or add things. We knew we had fought a battle that was old, and we had lost.

XV

Student Passed Out

Once, I was working in a class in Santa Monica. The students were in a semi-circle around me. I was looking straight ahead focused on a young man whose skin looked very pale. I soon noticed him sweating and his eyes becoming unfocused.

He was no longer drawing. I watched as he listed to one side, falling against the student next to him and then completing the fall onto the floor. The student on his side didn't even look over at him, being so concentrated on drawing. No one seemed to even notice. Not knowing if it was appropriate for the model to talk, I blurted out, "That guy just passed out!"

All the students turned to him, freaking out, not knowing what to do. The instructor had left the room momentarily. The young woman next to him not only seemed to know what to do but knew him. She reached into his backpack and pulled out a syringe, deftly injected him and patted his back until he came to.

"This happens all the time when he doesn't eat properly," she told us. "He's a diabetic and went into shock."

I was relieved that it wasn't my pose that was the cause. The poor guy was disoriented and embarrassed, but the rest of the class continued on. The instructor walked back in totally unaware of what had just happened.

XVI

Is She Smiling?

    The second time I modeled was for a painting class at UCLA. At that time my vision was so bad that I had to put my glasses on to see my face in the morning. I also had to tap around with my hands to find them. The instructor wanted me to remove my glasses. I carefully put them on top of my robe, which was on a nearby chair. Since it was a painting class, I had to stay in the same position for three hours with breaks every 20 minutes or so. I was facing in the direction of one particular woman, who I thought kept smiling at me. I didn't know if I was allowed to smile back, or not, or if that would ruin their paintings, but I did go ahead and smile and smile and smile and smile. I wondered why she kept smiling at me. I thought maybe she knew I was new to modeling and just wanted to make me feel comfortable. I put on my glasses during each break. I would look over at her and smile, but she seemed to be ignoring me. Later on, during one of my last breaks, I had my glasses on and looked over at her. She was working very hard on her painting, and with equally bad eyesight she was squinting to see the background of where I had been posing.

Oh, so that's what she had been doing all along! I must have looked like such a grinning fool, smiling and smiling and smiling back at her.

XVII

Up on a Rock in L.A.

Reclining Pose
Greta

In Los Angeles, I worked for a very sensual woman painter. Her paintings of food were erotic. We clicked well together, as I'm a bit of a foodie. She appreciated my Renoir-type body and often hired me for her classes. One day, she decided to take her class out on a picnic. We all went trekking up to the mountains, which started out as a nice, warm summer day. The instructor brought salami, bread, pickles and a gallon, or two, of wine. When we got to a quiet spot close to where a friend of hers lived, I disrobed and climbed up onto a rock with the help of some of the students. I basically was basking in the sunlight, getting a tan while the students drew me. Los Angeles was great for that.

After about an hour, we heard a helicopter circling and saw that it was the fire patrol. I was in a precarious position, unable to jump down quickly and put my clothes back on, so I just waved at them, as did the rest of the class. At my next break, we all decided we were famished and decided to gorge on the food. The students helped me down off the rock and I put my clothes back on. Then, we heard another helicopter circling. This time it was the police. We waved. They waved.

After the picnic, I went back up on the rock for another pose. On my next break, after I had put my clothes back on, we heard yet another helicopter. This time it landed. It was the sheriff. Everyone had time to cover up their drawings. The sheriffs, (two guys), were looking around hoping to see the nude woman they had heard about. They looked disappointed to see a bunch of innocent-looking people just sitting around. So, then they started to feel their oats asking us who was under twenty-one and drinking alcohol and why were there so many cars parked in the fire road, and other bullshit, etc. As it happened, only the teacher, her friend and I were over 21, but they were so disappointed at not having found the nude woman that they decided to leave after telling us we had to leave, as well. Our offense: parking in the fire road.

XVIII

Perspective

After having modeled for a while and listening to various art teachers, I got itchy to try drawing. When I was much younger, I wasn't too bad at it. I even drew a picture of a Heinz 57 Catsup bottle and sent it in for a prize for my little sister, Sharon. The ad on our black and white TV said to draw the picture and send in a picture of yourself (I sent in my sister's picture) and they would send back a doll with your face on it. Nothing ever came in the mail, but I worked on it for a few days and was sure my sister would get a doll that looked exactly like her. I gave up after a month of waiting for the mailman.

I thought it would be cool to be on the other end of the artist modeling experience, so I took an art class at UCLA. I was the only student who couldn't see what they call "perspective". This was obvious when I tried to park my car or find an address. I wasn't the worst student in the class, but I, for sure, wasn't in the top ten.

This perspective thing became more obvious as time went on. A memory that often amuses me is that after I had been modeling for a few months, I walked by an open door where the model was on the stand. I was shocked!

Oh my God! They can see everything!

Bonne Anniversaire
Nancy Gotthart

I'm not sure if this had to do with my lack of spatial awareness, but I had no idea of what the students could really see. This didn't stop me, only gave me pause.

One instance of my lack of perspective was when I was modeling for a class at UCLA and brought a parasol, thinking it would be a very cool prop. I sat myself up on a stool, opened the parasol and faced the wall. In my mind, it was a beautiful pose. The instructor, an Englishman, walked around to the front of me, looked me in the eye and said, "Hello, Luv. I just wondered if you wanted the students to see you?" I was confused. "What?" He politely cleared his throat and said, "Your lovely parasol is covering up your entire body from the back." *Oh, oops!* I blushed and turned myself around. That's what I mean. *Perspective.*

XIX

Modeling for Each Other in Santa Monica

Posing
Anonymous

Some of the models decided to get together on Sunday afternoons and draw each other. We met in Santa Monica in an apartment upstairs. The guy who lived downstairs was a potter and a really nice guy, so we invited him too. After we had been meeting for several months, my parents bought property in Big Sur and were getting rid of unwanted items in their house in Los Angeles. For their 25th wedding anniversary, they were given a vase, rather large, bigger than a breadbox, which they promptly hid behind the living room couch because it was so ugly. It was a greyish green color and looked like whoever had designed it had rolled up the clay like snakes and wrapped it around from the bottom to the top. This item was handed to me by my father, who said, "Can you just give this to one of your artist friends?"

"Okay, Daddy. I'll try."

That Sunday, I wrapped the vase up in my red button-down cardigan, put it in the back seat of my red 1966 VW Bug, and drove to Santa Monica. I got to the drawing-group meeting early because I wanted to see if I could give the vase away to the potter from downstairs. Leaving it in the car, I climbed the steps to the upstairs apartment and walked in to find Jill and Michael there. Jill was the model who rented the upstairs and Michael was the potter. The conversation ensued like this:

"So, Michael, my parents got this hideously ugly vase for their 25th wedding anniversary, which they hid behind the couch in the living room for at least five years. Now, they're moving, and my dad asked me to try and get rid of it by giving it to one of my 'artist friends.' I figured since you're a potter, maybe you could take a look at it and possibly fix it or something."

Michael, who was sitting on a stool, looked at me with a puzzled look on his face.

"Sure, I'll look at it. But where is it?"

"Oh, I left it in my car. Just understand that I didn't give this thing to them. I had nothing to do with it."

"Okay."

I went to my car, carefully grabbed the vase wrapped up in my red sweater and ascended the steps once more. Upon entering, I thrust the vase, sweater included, at Michael. He unwrapped it slowly, put the sweater on the table in front of him and held the vase in his hands. Rocking back and forth on the stool, he turned it upside down and started to howl.

"What's so funny?"

Michael looked at me, bemused.

"You know who made this vase?"

"No. Of course not."

There was a pause as he giggled.

"I did!"

"What?"

"I made this vase and I think it's beautiful!"

I started to apologize, as he held up his hand and shook his head.

"Don't worry about it. I'm going to resell it."

The next two hours as we were drawing each other, whenever our eyes met, we'd chortle. What are the odds?

XX

Anton - Atypical Hookup

Most of the time modeling was not an erotic trip for me. However, there is one time that stands out in my mind as an outstanding exception.

I had a job at Otis Art Institute and was in the middle of my first pose when I began looking around at the students, as I usually did with my peripheral vision. I saw a man in a tank top with a chiseled face and body. He was so fucking handsome. I could hardly believe it. Being awestruck, I did all my poses facing him (not my usual M.O.). During my break, I put my clothes back on and sat on the steps outside of the school. He walked over to me and started talking in a delicious Slavic accent. I could hardly believe he was talking to me, let alone with this accent. I have a weakness for foreign accents.

Anton: I have need of model. (Slavic accent)
Me: Oh, you do?
Anton: Private model.
Me: (I could hardly talk) mmhmm.

Anton: I vould like to use you. Is okay?

Me: Yeah. Sure.

Anton: Can we use your house? My vife, she gets jealous.

Me: Okay. (Eight million thoughts go whizzing through my mind.) Here's my address.

Here was the trip. I was crashing at a friend of mine's house on his service porch. Also, there was this other guy crashing there, an incredible nerd. I didn't really want to model when either of them were around. First of all, I would have been too embarrassed, and second of all, so would they. So, I arranged for Anton (who turned out to be from Yugoslavia) to come and draw me during the day, when both of them would be gone. Needless to say, I was very nervous with horny excitement the day he arrived. I must add at this point that he was quite an accomplished artist. He started drawing me and was sitting close enough so that I could see his drawing.

On one hand, the fact that I could see his drawing was good because I could keep my eye on his drawing and not on him. But then again, he was sitting very close to me. He kept giving me this lustful grin and I kept pretending that he was just smiling. I wasn't having much success at believing my own bullshit. After about three 20-minute poses, as I was taking a 5-minute break...

Anton: You have noticed maybe a look of desire on my face?

Me: (staring at the floor intently) I guess so.

Anton: I'm strong like bull.

Me: Oh.

At this point I got up on my knees (I had been sitting). I started walking on my knees over to the door. He grabbed me, kissed me and looked me in the eyes.

Anton: Vat is wrong vis that?

Me: (melting) Nothing.

We then proceeded to go the service porch and fuck our brains out. I'm usually not a very spontaneous person, so this was very exciting. Anyway, right in the middle of going at it, he looked down at me and said,

Anton: You like fuck?
Me? What?
Anton: You like fuck?
Me: (embarrassed) Yes.
Anton: Say fuck.
Me: What?
Anton: Say fuck.
Me: (relenting and feeling ridiculous) fuck.

After that, or should I say when we finished fucking some more, he grinned at me and said,

Anton: You were good.
Me: So were you. (amused)

Then we got dressed and went into the living room. He went on a long-winded discussion about how he was a great artist and was going to be famous and travel around the country. Then, he went on about how he was a Communist and blah, blah, blah. He seemed to want me to join him in this intellectual bullshit, but all I could concentrate on was how good I felt and how erotic the last hour had been. I couldn't have given a shit about his fucking political views or whether he was taking a trip to Timbuctoo. He finally realized I wasn't particularly interested in his discussion and wanted to pay me for modeling. An argument ensued and it was long. I didn't want his money. I felt awkward accepting it after all that happened. The business had turned to pleasure. He kept going on and on about how I had worked hard as a model and had done three poses, etc. He finally threw the money on the table and walked out. I never saw him again.

I heard later that he had seduced almost every artist model who worked at Otis Art Institute during his stay in the United States.

I was amused but did get tested at the free clinic for syphilis and the clap.

One thing about going to free clinics was that no matter what walk of life we were in—rich, poor, whatever—we were all there together for the same thing. We sat in embarrassed silence in folding chairs, looking down at the floor, waiting for our name to be called so we could first see a "counselor" and tell him, or her, who we had been with, and then go to another room to get tested. At this one, when they called the name of a cool-looking African American dude, he sauntered up to the front, turned to us with a sly grin and announced, "No matter what we do, we's cool!" and then he tipped his imaginary hat. We all burst out laughing at that and began to talk to each other.

XXI

Learning While Modeling

One of the great pleasures of being an artist model is getting a vicarious art education. I feel as if I've had eight years of drawing, painting and sculpture instruction from some of the best teachers in California. Another benefit is having the honor to work for famous artists and sometimes getting to know them personally. I did get to work for Richard Diebenkorn at UCLA. It wasn't a lot of fun though. He had me get inside a few cardboard boxes, so the students only saw my arms and legs protruding out. Not much creativity for me. In general, though, how else would you just get to sit quietly in a creative atmosphere, looking at people one by one, all of whom are giving you their full attention, and get paid for it?

XXII

Beginning Artists

    Thinking about faces, sometimes an interesting thing happens, especially for beginning artists who are learning to draw or paint. As I said before, people often apologize to the models about their abilities. That is very sweet. I've learned not to take it personally, ever. What did happen, and I noticed it more than once, was that beginning artists drew what they were used to seeing. They drew a version of themselves. That's who they saw in the mirror every day. It takes a while to learn to really see what you are looking at. There had been occasions where I looked at their drawings or paintings, and it looked exactly like them.

XXIII

A Booking Worth Forgetting

Once, I did get very bored when, for who knows what reason, I was hired for a business-college class in fashion design. The instructor thought it would be good for them to draw the nude, for the experience. I looked at their drawings after my first pose. They had drawn me like a stick figure with a turned-up nose and straight hair. *Um, no.* After that, I was totally turned off. That was the only time that ever happened. I have a Renoir-esque type of body, very curly hair, and a prominent Roman-esque nose. *Ahem.*

XXIV

Art Teachers' Styles

This world of artist modeling was an adventure I was more than willing to undertake. There was something about not knowing what to expect, other than that I would most likely be appreciated, that appealed to me. The '70s was an age of experimentation, and I soon learned that art teachers seemed to be on the cutting edge.

Louis Lunetta, an art teacher whom I had dated in the recent past, decided he wanted to see what the students would do if another painting teacher and I showed up on the first day of class, and while he was pretending to be a student, he got into a verbal argument over who was the real teacher. Roberto Chavez was the other "teacher", a very cool Chicano dude. Then we were both supposed to be incensed that another imposter was acting like *they* were the real teacher. Then, we were supposed to pretend that we were going to march off to the administration building and demand that they clear up the problem. When we stormed out, the real teacher, Louis, riled up the students and got them to sign a paper voting who they wanted as their real teacher. We came back in just as he admitted to them that yes, in fact, he was the real teacher. Some of the students didn't believe him. Some were perplexed.

Some were angry. The next week when I came in to be the model, I felt very uncomfortable disrobing after having pretended to be the teacher and duping them. The students were on edge, both with me and the instructor. I'm not sure if he got the response he was hoping for.

XXV

What It Takes

At parties, when I told people what I did for a living, they often looked at me in disbelief. Sometimes, when people used to ask me what I did and I told them, their eyebrows would raise, their eyes widen and the question "Does your mother know you do that?" might be blurted out. Or, they might say, "Does your husband approve?" or "How could anyone want to do that?" It definitely isn't for everyone. You find out in the first few hours whether you are or are not that kind of person.

I knew a woman who thought she'd try being an artist model. The first time she worked, a man kept drawing her crotch. She felt uneasy and kept moving away, only to have him move closer and continue to draw her crotch. She excused herself, went to the bathroom and threw up. That ended her modeling career.

And then, there was the occasional male model who would get a hard-on while he was modeling. He'd excuse himself, run to the bathroom to pour cold water on the appropriate part of his body, and return. Once, this happened where there was a shower in the bathroom. When this guy returned, his penis was dripping with soap.

This was not going well. When he got another woody, he yelled defiantly at the students and teacher saying he was a good model, a very good model, that he was just having a bad day and if anyone wanted, he'd give them his phone number so he could model for him. No one accepted his offer. Surprise.

Speaking of hard-ons, most of the male models I knew somehow had a way to take care of that issue. Or, if on occasion it happened, they told me it was just part of life. If the students were going to feel uncomfortable, that was their problem.

When I would model with a male model, it wasn't usually a problem. Most of them were gay, so modeling with a woman wasn't an issue.

XXVI

Expectations

How's This?
Anonymous

There seemed to be an unwritten law about not letting the model know if he/she turned you on. I found that unfortunate sometimes when, in fact, I was available and horny. If I wanted to break the ice, I had to initiate it. In an art class, where they may be thirty students, the mystique of being nude is already laid bare, so to speak, and the sexual vibe, if there is one, doesn't last long. The students are concentrating too much on light, shadow, perspective and form to think about anything else. They are learning to see. The only students who broke that rule were the occasional math or anthropology students who happened to take a drawing class for fun. There's another unwritten law that says you can't touch the model. That's probably a good rule, in most cases. This not-putting-out-a-sexual vibe was true in my case. (Not in everyone's, as you'll read later.) As far as vibes were concerned, I often thought of Art Deco, which I admired, and tried to imitate it with the geometric patterns.

XXVII

Kinds of Poses and Preferences

I preferred the 10-second to 5- or 10-minute poses. These allowed for a lot of exercise and creativity, which made the time pass very quickly. I could feel graceful and/or humorous during the short poses.

Some of the models who like to do long poses get into long fantasy trips or even hypnotize themselves. Some of them meditate. But I'm way too nosy. I didn't want to miss anything that might be happening between the students. Many people have asked me, "Don't you get bored?" *Hardly ever.* If there was just one interesting person in the room, I didn't get bored. When I posed, I tried to exude a feeling of playfulness or seriousness, basically whatever struck my fancy that day. If there was one person who picked up on that feeling, then my mission had been accomplished and I felt gratified. I felt like a kind of midwife. It was very gratifying when it worked.

Sometimes sitting on the stand for long periods of time lent itself to fantasizing about trips that I wanted to take or had taken.

XXVIII

Musing While on the Stand

Passport Photo 1972

London

After modeling for six months in Los Angeles, I decided to make the big trip to Europe. I saved all my money ($2,000) and ended up going alone after a few vague promises from people who said they wanted to accompany me but didn't follow through. The first month in London was great. I had acquired a sweetie almost overnight.

The way it actually happened was that I sat next to an American guy on the plane, who said he had friends in London and that we could crash there. Once we had made our way to Earl's Court, we sat on the stoop of the flat belonging to his "friends" and waited for them to come home. He had bought some fish and chips on the way and didn't even offer to share them with me. I hadn't realized yet that I needed to have some English money.

About five minutes after we had begun sitting on the stoop, the window of the apartment next door opened up and a couple of really groovy hippies handed us a joint. Joints in Europe at that time were made of hash and tobacco and they were about 6-inches long. I was not a tobacco smoker, but hey, it was a gift. When his friends got back, they were hospitable and not surprised at the visit. Their house had been a kind of crash pad for various people who were traveling. The two guys who lived there and paid rent were named Ian and Keith. Ian was from Scotland. Keith was from London. They were house painters. They never asked for any money. The American guy assumed I was going to sleep with him that first night. *Um, no.* I rolled out my sleeping bag on the floor next to Ian's single bed. Ian got into his bed and said to me,

"It's rather cold here, don't you think?"

"Huh?"

I didn't get the hint. I'd never heard a line like that before.

"I said, It's rather cold in here."

I remained unable to get his real meaning. He basically had to spell it out for me.

"Would you fancy coming up here with me and keep me warm?"

Ohhhh. Hmm. What an offer. Since I was afraid I'd be hassled by the American guy who wouldn't share his fish and chips, and Ian was so kind and unassuming, not to mention nice-looking, I agreed. I became his temporary girlfriend overnight. We never did have much privacy, as there were always various travelers staying at their flat.

During one of the weeks that I stayed in that flat, a large man named Morton with a red velvet cape announced that he'd just come from Katmandu and whipped his cape around his body. He looked around the flat and found a unique place to sleep, the clawfoot bathtub.

I asked him, "Are you comfortable?"

"Perfectly, Luv."

One night, everyone in the household had gone to a Jimi Hendrix concert. Ian and I thought this was our chance to get it on in private. Someone had left a bowl of what we assumed was hash and proceeded to smoke it. We put on a Jimi Hendrix LP on the record player in the room. Pretty soon, my head felt like it was three or four times larger than it was. *One pill makes you larger and one pill makes you small.* The song on the record was over, but the thought of walking the three feet to the record player to turn it over seemed to be an impossible feat. We both just lay there stoned out of our heads, so to speak.

I stayed in Ian and Keith's flat for about a month, cooking them dinners, wandering around London, buying Cadbury bars and trying not to get lost. I told Ian and Keith that I wanted to travel around Europe. They said they had friends who also had a crash pad in Amsterdam, and I just had to meet the guy who decided who could live in the house, have some kind of interview to see if I was a good fit for their community, and then I'd have a home base.

Amsterdam

I decided to take Ian and Keith up on their offer and made my way over to the Netherlands. The first day I got to Amsterdam, I stayed in the youth hostel for a day or two until I got up the nerve to go to the address Ian and Keith had given me. I found the house and walked up the rickety stairs into a room with giant windows. The Dutch didn't mind at all if people looked into their business. They never put curtains on windows, as far as I could tell. On New Year's Eve, the custom was to throw any unwanted furniture out of the windows. One had to be careful walking down the streets that night at midnight. They were a very open-minded and curious people, unlike paranoid Americans.

The building I had the address for was behind Dam Square, near the red-light district (legal brothels). It was condemned. The first big room I saw had about five people living in it, who were the people I was to live with, if they let me. All the angles in the building were amiss. I guessed that the house was settling into the canals or something like that. There no longer existed right angles. I never was sure that I wasn't on a tilt when I was inside. But, then again, I was stoned most of the time anyway, on hash, tobacco, or opium. I had not been a cigarette smoker before I went to Europe, but as I said, all the joints in Europe were made of hash and tobacco. So, what's a poor girl to do?

I walked into the room feeling rather insecure, but hopeful. The room was big and at one end was a man quietly talking with the little girl, who looked to be around five years old. This older man who lived there decided to take on the responsibility of being the little girl's surrogate father. It seemed like her mother was one of the housemates, and the father wasn't in the picture. So, this man just took over. The shocking thing about him was his appearance. He never wore anything but a shirt. When I first got to the house, I had to be interviewed by him. He made the decisions about who could stay and who couldn't. When I walked in, I saw him sitting cross-legged on the floor making things out of leather with nothing but an undershirt on and talking softly to a little girl. I couldn't believe it. He had coarse, red, wiry hair all over his body, kind, reddish-brown eyes and a Yorkshire accent, just walked around with his cock and balls dangling and thought nothing of it. He was at once kind, rebellious, ornery, and fatherly.

He was mostly very good with his "adopted" little girl. He would never spank her or yell at her. He would quietly ask her to come over to him, if she did something wrong, and quietly wait for her to admit it, softly asking her to apologize. He was gentle and strong and very vehement about letting her have a lot of freedom. I supposed this freedom was good up to a point but letting her defecate in the street was over the top for me. His name was Peter.

The little girl's name was Terry. She had a Yorkshire accent like her mother, Sue, who lived in the house with her current boyfriend and would talk about when she was "in 'ospital" in England. When Peter or Terry's mother would swear, they would say, "fuckin' 'ell." Terry, of course, picked up this expression and would walk around saying, "fuckin' 'ell" and "want some shit?" "Shit" meaning marijuana or hashish. Terry, like her mother, had dark brown eyes and hair. Sue once told me in a hushed whisper that she was Jewish. An ex-junkie, she had been put into the hospital to kick the habit. While she was there, her daughter was taken away from her and put in a children's home. When she got out of the hospital, she stole Terry from the home and came to Amsterdam, hoping they wouldn't find her. Peter came with her. They had been lovers at one time, with Peter taking over being both the mother and the father, when Sue couldn't handle it.

Although Sue was now in love with and living with an American guy name Bob, Peter was willing, apparently with no ill feelings, to stay there and parent Terry in the same room with his old girlfriend and her new boyfriend. In the household there was also a Portuguese soldier who had run away, and with a few other stray people who constantly moved in and out of the that room. Terry's mother wasn't very good at disciplining her or taking care of her needs, so Peter more or less worked out perfectly.

My initiation or acceptance into the house was to be decided by Peter. He took me for a walk with Terry and we talked for a while. I don't remember what we talked about. I remember feeling a little anxious, whether I would "make the grade" or not. The thought of staying in the youth hostel wasn't too appealing. But mainly, it was a nice walk with an interesting, fuck-the-straight-world-and-society-in-general guy with his ornery ideas, that I couldn't help agreeing with. By the way, he did put on pants to walk in the street, but no shoes. The next day, I learned that I had passed the test and moved in.

The American guy named Bob who was currently Sue's lover was another charismatic character. He had a head full of frizzy, dark brown hair and soft, dark brown eyes. He had an earring in one ear (very fashionable at the time) and was very thin. The main thing about him was his instant attraction to people, especially women. He was gentle, soft, kind, and very affectionate, and treated women with respect. He was like a bona fide flower child. He believed in fighting wars of any kind with love, and he was very successful. He had lived in Europe for many years, going back to the States, once in a while, to visit close friends. He also had an endearing chip in one of his front teeth. He smoked a lot of dope and wrote poetry. He and Sue had a makeshift curtain around their bed. When they wanted to make love, they just pretended nobody could see or hear. Their loving each other was very reassuring in a way.

I set up my sleeping bag on the floor in the middle of the room, trying to put as much space between myself and everyone else as possible. I supposed that space amounted to about five feet on all sides.

The other person who occupied the room and brought food for everyone was a sixteen-year-old girl from the Dutch West Indies. She was small, dark, and strikingly beautiful with great soulful eyes and colorful gypsy clothes. She read fortunes and supported most of us with the money she got from the government. Her mother had been in and out of mental hospitals since she was three years old. She had never known her father. She had grown up fast and formed her own very sound philosophy of life, learning to fend for herself in any way she could, which included lying and stealing.

The girl had to go see a social worker once a week and promise not to smoke hash or trip on acid. If she did this, she was given a check. She'd buy a lot of food and a lot of hash and turn us on to any other treats she found. She wasn't always there, because of a torrid love affair with another character who lived on a houseboat in a nearby canal. She talked about the rhythms of life and space. She had lived alone and had to support herself since she was eleven. She seemed very wise to me.

The whole house had one bathroom, or, I should say, a small closet with a toilet in it. There was not always toilet paper. We would try to steal the toilet paper, whenever we could, usually from the youth hostel around the corner. That youth hostel also provided us with our only showers, when we could sneak by the main desk upstairs to use them. The best way to do that was to take Terry with us and ask if we could give our little girl a shower. She hated showers, but she went there at least three times a week with different people from the house. The people who lived next door to us allowed us to hook up our electricity to theirs. The room with the toilet in it usually stank so bad, I could hardly stand it. Having to climb a flight of rickety, tiny Dutch stairs to get to it only to find the door closed was another drag.

There was a kitchen on our floor, and we used a hot plate to warm up the usual meal of brown rice and vegetables. Other people in the house would sometimes bring home treats, like chocolate bars and cheese, or, if we were really lucky, we could share this sort of pudding in liquid form called "*Vanillafla*", or something like that. Someone else would get fresh baked bread, whether they stole it or bought it. The next important thing was the tobacco and papers to roll joints. Joints, European style, were rolled with five papers. They were long and conical, mixed half-and-half with tobacco and hashish. This was a harsh reality for me, and I became addicted to tobacco for six months because of it.

While in Amsterdam and living the hippy communal life, I decided to try modeling there. I asked around and found out that it was a drag to model for the local art school. You had to wait in a line outside the classroom, then the teacher would come out, look at all the prospective models and pick one. Can you imagine? So, I went to an art-supplies store and asked the man behind the counter if he knew of anyone who used models. He told me of a man who was an ambassador, or something like that from some country, and used models all the time. He gave me the man's number. I contacted the "Ambassador" and went and saw his God-awful cheesecake kind of paintings, but decided, "What the hell." He kept asking me about my lifestyle, chortling at the fact that I was living with about 30 other people in this one abandoned house. He kept trying to pump me for information about how the "hippies" lived. He assumed that everybody fucked everybody all the time and that it was one continuous orgy. Boy, was he wrong.

The second time I worked for him, he began patting me on the knee and offering me grapefruits and chocolate bars. I kept taking his slimy little paws off me and refusing the treats. Then, he asked me if he could come over to where I lived. (Heh, heh.) I'm sure he thought he would get laid the second he walked in the door. Then, he started giving me the tired old story about his wife being boring or something. (Yawn.)

I thought it might be funny to have him come there. I told him he could come upstairs, if he wanted, but that I couldn't model for him anymore. It was beginning to feel creepy. He never did show up.

Some of the people who lived in our abandoned house were pretty interesting, many of them younger than I was. I was 22 at the time. A guy who was older than me had his own room upstairs. He was Hungarian and had been in and out of jail a few times. He was inventing his own astrology. He asked each person who lived there to do a drawing. He provided us with pencils or colored crayons. Then, he'd ask us all kinds of questions about our lives. I guess he categorized our answers and put our drawings on his walls. He had great wallpaper. I think he was about 35, or so. He had very dark hair, intense dark eyes, and kept his room spotless.

There were many other people in that house, including the Portuguese deserter from the army and another English girl who was a kleptomaniac. The police would come up once in a while looking for Dutch runaways, but they would leave the rest of us alone.

Traveling Farther South

I decided after a month to tour the rest of Europe. It had been different and enlightening to live in that house in Amsterdam, but I was left with a gnawing feeling of loneliness.

A Dutch guy had flagged me down on the street in Amsterdam saying he recognized me from the plane coming from Los Angeles to London. He asked me if I wanted to go with him to Tangiers. I said, "Yes, of course!" I didn't really know where Tangiers was. I thought it was in Europe.

Traveling with Toon was an adventure. His sister drove us down to a truck stop on the southern tip of the Netherlands. We were to hitch a ride and see how far we could go without having to pay for a train. As I watched the huge, parked trucks, I saw a man with a belly about the size of an enormous pig get down from the driver's seat, take out a liter of some kind of soda with his left hand and hold his penis with his right hand. He proceeded to drink and piss at the same time. He was pissing directly onto one of the oversized tires. You may wonder what his cargo was. You guessed it. Pigs. In his truck, there were maybe 30 or 40 pigs piled on top of each other, oinking, pissing, and shitting. I looked at Toon and said, "There's no way I'm getting in that truck." Luckily, he agreed.

We got a ride in another big rig—one that didn't have pigs in the back—and got dropped off in Belgium. When we showed our passports to a woman in a small hotel, she wouldn't let us share a room because we weren't married. That was a shock. We just went to another one. No problem. Then, we got on a train that would end up at Malaga. Toon began exhibiting strange behavior in our hotel room and on the train. He had apparently taken LSD on his last night in Hollywood, about a month after he approached me in Amsterdam, and had never come down entirely. I could never know when he would suddenly have a flashback and begin caressing the seats or the couch.

This became annoying extremely fast. I felt like his nurse. We did not have a sexual relationship. I basically had to pry his hands loose from whatever he was fixated on and reassure him, and the people who may have been observing, that it was all under control. Not really.

When we got to Malaga, there was a very big ferry boat awaiting passengers to Tangiers.

"Why do we have to take a ferry?" I asked like a dumb American.

"Because we are going to Tangiers."

"Well, where is it?"

"In Morocco."

"In Morocco?"

"Yes."

"You mean, North Africa?"

"Yes."

"An entirely different continent?"

"Yes."

"Wow!"

There were a long line of hippies waiting to board the ferry. There was one problem, however. They weren't letting any longhairs into the country. I just happened to have a pair of scissors in my backpack and offered to give $5 haircuts. Once word got out that I was doing that, a long line formed with guys hoping to take the next ferry, which was leaving in about an hour. I didn't really know how to cut hair, but I tried my best to make it a kind of a shag look. I would say, "I don't really know what I'm doing." And they would say, "Go for it." I made $100 in about an hour. In my defense, I must say they didn't look horrible. Not great. But not horrible.

When we got to Tangiers, I was blown away by the noise level, the colors, people walking around in djellabas, speaking Arabic or French, beggars, strong, sweet mint tea, music, and hundreds of hippies like us.

We ended up on the beach where I had had just about enough

of Toon's flashbacks. I told him to call his sister because I was no longer willing to travel with him. He nodded sadly and said he understood.

I met several people my age who were going to a small village called Diabat. They invited me to come along. We all piled into a questionable bus with live and dead goats and chickens strapped to the roof. The dead goats banged on the windows when we made a turn. Every time we stopped, beggars would get on the bus with bruised babies in their arms. It was very hard to watch. I was told not to give them money, but I had to. When the bus stopped, it was pitch black outside. I have night blindness, so when I stepped down, I just stopped. I couldn't see anything. I could only hear murmuring in Arabic, and I could feel people brushing past me in djellabas. One of the new hippy friends realized I wasn't following them, came back, and took me by the arm.

I ended up sharing an adobe hut with a guy named Walter. Walter was a kind of East Coast preppy guy, about six feet tall, replete with a dark blue blazer, blond hair, and a satchel with a Canadian flag on it. He told me that Americans weren't well liked, and it was easier to have a Canadian flag plastered on his suitcase. In our hut, there was no toilet, no running water, and no kitchen. Just a room. There was a well, located a few hundred yards down a hill, and if we needed to attend to our bodily needs, we had to try and find a bush nearby. This took a little getting used to for me. I saw that the locals were staring at us while we did what we needed to do.

Someone would come around in the morning and sell us fresh baked bread. They also offered us eggs. That was kind of it, except for a kind of storefront from someone else's hut that had 1,000-year-old chocolate in it. I bought it, of course. It tasted like it was infused with camel dung—not that I had ever tasted camel dung, of course.

After a couple of days, I decided I wanted to go into a village on the coast called Essaouira. I really needed to take a shower. Essaouira had Turkish baths and was known as a place that hippies from all over the world congregated. I told Walter that I was going to go there and get couscous. I didn't really know what it was, but I heard it was a regional dish and was determined to try it. I told Walter that he just needed to gather a few twigs, so we could heat up some water and cook it when I got back.

The baths were wonderful, steamy. Oh, how good it felt to be clean again. And then, I went wandering around looking for this famous couscous. After asking several people, I was told that an old man around the corner sold herbs. They pointed to him, and I approached. He sat on the ground with many bags of herbs and spices in front of him, selling his wares. I recognized some of the herbs: cumin, garlic, onions, oregano, sage, and mint. The rest were a mystery. At the time, I spoke French, and I asked him if he had any couscous. He smiled a toothless grin and offered me a small bag. I paid him in American dollars. He was only too happy. I tried to keep the look of evil I saw in his eyes and the wicked grin on his gaunt face out of my mind and began the seven-kilometer trek back to Diabat.

I felt very proud of myself for not getting lost and for buying the treasured couscous. This pride was my undoing. When I got to our hut, Walter had not collected even one twig. I don't know what the hell he really did, but I was pissed. I went outside and broke off several twigs from a nearby bush. Walter had a lighter and we poured water from the well into a tin cup. Upon opening the paper sack and looking inside, Walter informed me that he would not take one bite of whatever that was. I, on the other hand, was adamant that even though it looked like hay, I was not only going to cook it, but eat it. Walter raised one blond eyebrow. "Good luck," said Mr. Preppy.

I put one tablespoon into my mouth and tried to swallow. Whatever it was scratched the hell out of my throat. Within an hour and for the next three days, I was hallucinating, vomiting, and shitting my brains out. *Error. Big error.* Honestly, I could have died. I have no idea what that was or what it was laced with, but I'm pretty sure it wasn't couscous.

When I was better, we hitchhiked into Casablanca with another couple. We were told that there were no youth hostels open, but a large woman with many jewels and a turban on her head offered the four of us a room in her hotel. What we didn't immediately know was that it was a brothel. Like most places in Morocco, it had open areas in the middle with pillars in front of the walls inside. As we were walking, I thought I saw something quickly hide behind a pillar. The next time I saw it, I turned quickly to see a woman propositioning Walter and David, the other guy traveling with us. I found this very funny and encouraged them to go for it. I think they were terrified. The hotel smelled like Lysol. Not pleasant at all, but we needed a place to sleep at least for the night.

Marrakesh was next on the agenda. This was the place with what we called the "run for your life toilets." They were basically a hole in the floor and a showerhead above with a chain that you yanked to flush whatever grossness appeared in the hole. The problem was that the water pressure was so intense that unless you basically were all zipped up and ready to run, you'd get your traveler's diarrhea all over yourself.

The good thing about traveling with Walter was that because he was tall and blond, the Moroccan boys followed him, not me. The bad thing was that he was so fucking curious and walked very fast. I was afraid to lose him, so I scurried to keep up, walking past hanging carcasses of meat and candies, which were hanging on ropes with insects buzzing around both of them. I had gotten very sick from paella in Malaga—and let's not forget the famous couscous, albeit that was my fault—so all I was willing to eat was yogurt and mint tea.

In Marrakesh, I switched traveling partners from Walter to the other American guy named David. We hitchhiked to Rabat and were dropped off with a promise of a ride to the border in Ceuta the next morning, if we just stayed at this Parisian man's house.

When we walked in with the three Moroccan boys who had given us the ride, the house was pink inside. There was a room set up for a band. The boys led us into the bedroom of the owner like we were American toys. The man was lying in a round pink bed, wearing a black, silk kimono. He had his hand on his heart. I never did find out why. David was very sick from dysentery. I told the Parisian man about David, and he asked his maid to make David an herbal drink that would cure him. Then, he waved us out of his bedroom.

David gratefully drank the tea that was offered and fell immediately asleep on the living room floor. I put my sleeping bag on the floor about a foot away from his. He unfortunately was out like a light. At one point, I fell asleep. After a bit, I felt what I thought might be a spider on my neck, and I brushed it away. It came back immediately. As I opened my eyes, I saw a hand of one of the boys and screamed. I couldn't think in French, not even English really. I just screamed. David snored away. I must have scared the boy off, because he never came back, but we didn't get our ride to the border as promised in the morning. We didn't see the kimono man either to thank him. David was cured. At least that was good. We just walked about a mile to the highway and put out our thumbs.

Eventually, a hippie bus picked us up. In the back, along with backpacks, was a pillowcase full of grass. They asked us to help them smoke it up because they had to get rid of it before Ceuta, which was a part of Spain from which we'd take a ferry to get to the mainland. Because it was Spain, and not Morocco, if you were caught with any drugs, you were given a year and a day in jail. On that extra day, they could easily give you another year unless you or your family had enough money to bribe yourself out of jail. I had bought a hash cookie on the street in Marrakesh. Like an idiot, I decided to eat it in its entirety before we got on the ferry to Spain. I was so stoned; I didn't care what happened to me. I basically wanted to die. We found a youth hostel that luckily was open, and I crashed for several hours.

Even though I was meeting people to travel with, I still felt lonely. This feeling continued for the next five months. To soothe my loneliness, I began eating everything I saw, usually late at night. I traveled to Greece, Spain, France, Germany, and Italy. I met a lot of people, but I was essentially in need of something else. I didn't know what. There were many exciting moments, some scary, and always an adventure. I continued to eat my way through Europe.

When I got to my aunt's house in Italy, I had just come from Morocco. She was living in an ex-President's house in Frascati. I hadn't seen anything so extravagant in months. Mostly, I had been staying in youth hostels or people's backyards. In that house, there was an actual bathtub and a full-length mirror. That evening, I took my first bath in about five months and was shocked as I gazed at the Rubenesque body in the mirror. Although I was in proportion, I was definitely a lot heavier, than I'd ever been. I looked like some of those paintings in the museums. This didn't cause me to stop eating too much, though. I ate Nutella and banana sandwiches for snacks and continued to gorge myself for the rest of my seven months in Europe.

When my mother saw me as I got off the plane back in California, she cried. She cried because she was happy to see me and because I had put on so much weight. I was miserable. I went back to Los Angeles paranoid and unhappy. Everyone commented on my weight. I was greatly appreciated by the students who drew me, but I couldn't even accept that. I decided that the man I had left, to go to Europe could never stand me now that I was so fat, and Los Angeles suddenly seemed claustrophobic. I heard about the San

Francisco Models Guild and found out that the auditions were in a week. I went for it.

XXIX

Modeling in the Bay Area

San Francisco

I made the decision to move to the Bay Area and found a place with Beth, a model friend of mine, and her boyfriend, Howard, from L.A. She wanted to make lots of money and worked as an exotic dancer in a sleazy joint near our apartment in Oakland, California. She used to parade around the apartment all the time with just her G-string and tassels on, gazing at herself in the mirror whenever she couldn't get anyone else to admire her. I, of course, was still overweight because of basically eating Europe and was jealous of her lithe body. Her flaunting it really made me sick. She'd call me into the bathroom to show me how much weight she'd lost and ask me how many fleabites she had on her back and the backs of her legs. Besides all that, she'd bring home middle-aged men from the club and would make out with them in the same bed she shared with her boyfriend. Most of the time, he was even there, sulking in the kitchen.

At that time, I had a waterbed. Howard had a cat, Mazie. Cats and waterbeds don't always make good companions. I realized this, when Mazie clawed a hole in my bed. Every time I leaned a bit on it, water would form a little puddle. My bedroom was directly across the hall from the bathroom, and in my oh-so-logical mind, I thought I could lift that waterbed out of its frame and pour it out in the clawfoot bathtub across the hall. *Er, no.* So, one early morning at 2 a.m. I decided I'd had enough water on my elbows and tried to lift the waterbed out of the frame. Howard heard me struggling and came to help.

"No, Helene. You can't lift a waterbed. It weighs a ton."

"But Mazie clawed a hole in it."

"Sorry about that. Okay. Listen, I'll attach a hose to it and go down to the driveway and siphon the water out."

We lived on the second floor on 41st near Telegraph. This street at that time was a bit sketchy: fights, glass breaking, ambulances, etc. Howard attached the hose and we tossed it out of my bedroom window to the driveway. Then, he lay down on his back and attempted to siphon the water out. It wasn't working. Not remembering what time it was, or how loud I was, I yelled out the window, "SUCK HARDER, Howard!"

Immediately, lights were flicked on and windows opened in the apartment building next door. Howard was holding his stomach, giggling. He did in fact need to suck harder. When he did, it worked.

After many weeks of Beth prancing around in her getup and bringing men home, Howard and I finally kicked her out. Then, like a sap, he moved right next door to her, so he could suffer even more, as he watched her bring someone new home night after night.

XXX

Ford

Being in the San Francisco Models Guild was mostly a lot of fun. We were a big crazy family. I got to work with some of them on occasion and it was never dull. One of the models in the San Francisco Models Guild was a prankster. His name was Ford. Ford was tall, way over 6 feet. He had long everything: face, hair, arms, legs, and nose. He always wore John Lennon-shaped sunglasses and occasionally, a red sequined penis ring. Very festive.

Once, when we were double-booked at the De Young Museum in San Francisco, he really got me, but good. The teacher had set up a dark green cloth, which he backlit so that the models who were behind it were in silhouette. He asked Ford and I to do four 5-minute poses, two 10-minute poses and one 20-minute pose behind the cloth screen. I should have known by the smirk he had on that Ford would try to embarrass the hell out of me, but I was oblivious. For one of the 5-minute poses, I got on the floor on my knees and did a back bend with my body arched up towards the ceiling. Ford, upon seeing this pose of mine, stood at least three feet behind me, bending over, stretching his long arms down and his long, bony fingers clamped together as if picking cherries. Alas, it wasn't cherries he was picking; it was my nipples.

As he was three feet behind me, he wasn't touching me at all, but the students couldn't tell. To them, it looked as if he was really pinching my nipples. With my head falling backwards, I couldn't exactly say much, but I muttered under my breath, "Ford! Goddam it! Cut that out!" His response was, "Whatever do you mean?" On our break, after I put on my robe, I was too mortified to come out from behind the screen to look at the drawings, like I usually did. I just stayed back there and fumed. When the class was over, I was forced to come out from behind the screen. The students had their faces turned towards their drawings. They seemed as embarrassed as me.

XXXI

The Guild and Flo Allen

As I said, being a member of the San Francisco Models Guild was pretty exciting for me. After a few memorable meetings, I was interested in the history.

The Guild had been in existence since 1946. One of the founders was Florence Allen, an African-American voluptuous version of Mae West. She was considered a legend. During the '70s, there was hardly an artist over 30 in the Bay Area who hadn't drawn or painted her. There was a full-page article on her in the *San Francisco Chronicle* in October 1978. She had modeled over 30 years. Like others who had modelled for a long time, she had a show with all the drawings and paintings she had received over the years.

When she first started, the wages were 50 to 75 cents an hour, which, in her words, were "big bucks in those days." At the time of the article, the hourly wage had gone up to a whopping $4.00 an hour. She even taught a class at the California College of Arts and Crafts on how to model. One of the many quotes in the article that resonates with me was about size and shapes of models. Artist models are not fashion models. It's a different kind of beauty altogether. Flo said, "Besides, the art students don't like the pretty, pretty ones. They like them when they've got a lot of stuff on them. The, uh, fuller figure."

When I first met Flo, I was warned that she was sometimes difficult to get along with. I wanted to get some work from her. She booked the models for the California College of Arts and Crafts (CCAC). At this time in her life, she only modeled on special occasions for special people. I was given the address of a house in Oakland. I walked up some steps and when I opened the door, there was no mistaking which person was Flo Allen. She was sitting at her desk, wearing a loud, snug-fitting dress, high heels, lots of bright jewelry and long, long false eyelashes. I liked her immediately.

She gave me a short interview and told me that she didn't need any more models. I was pissed. I got up very quickly and started to walk out. She called me back and said, "Sit down. I can tell by the way you walk that you're a good model." She then proceeded to give me lots of work. She admonished me for not wearing a bra. (this was in the '70s; many of us had stopped wearing bras). She told me I'd be sorry when my breasts would be droopy as I got older. She said the reason her breasts were still beautiful was because she always wore a bra. In later years, I saw her at an art opening where I was taking Polaroid pictures of people. She was very friendly and very onstage. It was sad to see her at that time because she was walking with a cane, a beautiful, fallen idol.

I worked for her for a good while, the two of us exchanging haughty comments with each other, like "How'd you like working in that dungeon?" "Oh, I hope I can work there every day." Then, the usual thing occurred. I say "usual" because I had been warned that this would happen. One thing about Flo was that she was great as a person to talk to, but to work together was another thing altogether.

She wasn't exactly organized. What had happened in the past was that a model wouldn't show up for a job that Flo had forgotten to book. The model would get blamed and wouldn't get much work after that. The administration of the schools had so much fear and respect for Flo that they chose to believe her, no matter what.

I got the phone call once while I was in Katy's guest bedroom. A lot of hanky-panky went on in that house. For instance, when I was about to hop in the sack with a man who happened to be my dentist, and hardly able to concentrate considering what she had disturbed, I listened as Flo started yelling at me for not showing up to a job, for which she had never booked me. That phone call ruined our relationship, and I never worked for her again. And, in case you're wondering, the fling with the dentist never was consummated.

To be a booking agent for models is a very hard job. Sometimes there are difficult instructors. They can be absent-minded and head-strong. They have been known to call up the booking agent at the last minute, demanding a certain model. Of course, the booking agent also has a lot of power. If she or he doesn't like a certain model, the response to a request might be "they are not available." Models who weren't in the Guild sometimes had a hard time, because if they wanted to work at CCAC or UC Berkeley, they would have to kiss the ass of the models' booking agent unless they could sneak around and get the teacher to hire them directly. If they did that and were caught by the models' secretary, they incurred a wrath unlike any other.

XXXII

Katy and Nancy in Noe Valley

Katy and Froggy in her Bedroom
Anonymous

I will be forever grateful to Katy and Nancy for coming to my rescue when I was working at the College of San Mateo and came down with the flu.. I felt so bad that I didn't think I could drive myself home. I called Nancy Gotthart, the Guild's booking agent, and asked her what I should do. Nancy told me that she and her partner, Guild President Katy Allen, would drive the forty-five minutes from their home in San Francisco, get me and my car, bring me back to their place, and nurse me back to health.

Ah, the comfort of women. I could hardly believe my ears. Here were two women I hardly knew, willing to transport me to their house and care for me.

Katy and Nancy lived in a two-story Victorian house that was blue and white with gold trim in the heart of colorful Noe Valley, just above the Castro District, the neighborhood that was home to many of San Francisco's gay men and women. Beyond an iron gate was a small garden with blooming camellias. Pink and black marble steps led up to the front door. As soon as we arrived, Katy and Nancy whisked me inside and up to their guest bedroom, which they called the "honeymoon suite", and put me to bed with tea, joints and honey. I hadn't realized until that moment how much I needed the mothering sounds and friendship they offered. When I woke up later, it was to something I'd never experienced before, a room that held beauty wherever I looked.

A few weeks later, I asked Katy and Nancy if I could visit again. Modeling was great, but I had started to feel lonely. I felt shy about reaching out to these two women socially, because I didn't feel like I was part of the in-group that they were the center of. But they were the only people I knew, besides my roommates, and I craved companionship.

It took some doing to find my way back to their house. I have always been directionally challenged. Whenever I would get lost on my way to modeling jobs, which was not infrequent, I would make a frantic phone call from a gas station or a phone booth, and Nancy, calmly as always, told me exactly how to get there. It would usually start out with, "Nancy! I'm lost!"

"What are the cross streets?"

"I don't know!"

"Take a deep breath. Get out of your car. Walk until you see street signs and tell me what they are."

"Oh. Okay."

But I found my way back to Katy and Nancy's Victorian for that first social visit, and any anxiety I may have had was quickly dispelled the moment I entered their museum-like home. In my feverish, flu-ridden state several weeks before, I hadn't really focused on the décor beyond the bathroom and the guest bedroom. But now, and for many years afterward, I became instantly stoned (metaphorically, as well as actually) when I walked into that house. It was like entering an ever-changing museum.

Since inheriting the house from Katy's grandmother, the two women had been filling it with antiques and *objets d'art*. The stairs leading up from the entry hall were covered in rose carpeting. The walls were filled with paintings, some of them Nancy's. Directly at the end of the hall was the kitchen, tiled in yellow, green, pink, red and blue. If that wasn't enough to dazzle one's brain, the wall above the Wedgewood stove sported several animal skulls, bleached white: a cow, a couple of horses, a goat and two weird small things that might have been rats. I was afraid to ask. Another wall featured a stuffed, baby alligator and two snakeskins. I didn't particularly care for them and tried to pretend they weren't there. Apparently, it was Katy who was into the skulls and the taxidermy. She often brought them with her to model as props. She carted around the stuffed chicken, the armadillo and the vulture when the mood struck her.

Atop the refrigerator sat two live doves in a cage. In the walk-in pantry was a window looking out on an impressionist painter's backyard and garden, somehow appearing both disarrayed and orderly, where Nancy grew all kinds of herbs and vegetables: comfrey, oregano, carrots, lettuce, potatoes and radishes. I was surprised that anything grew in the S.F. fog, but besides the edible garden, there were lemon verbena shrubs and bushes of fuchsias and camellias. I have a distinct memory of being in the kitchen with Katy, (stoned, of course) and watching her hold a head of lettuce as if it were a newborn. Then because she was making pate, she stuck the fingers of her left hand into a jar of raw liver, looked at me with half-lidded eyes and made a groaning with devilish pleasure noise.

To the left of the kitchen was the dining room; its walls papered in a French brick red, lushly adorned with gold birds, palm and banana leaves, and ivy. The chandelier, hanging over the dining table with its four goat-tit-shaped lamps, had been bought at an auction by Katy's grandmother; it had belonged to Sally Stanford, the famous S.F. Madame. Oh, and let me not forget the real, five-foot high, stuffed Roosevelt elk that inhabited the dining room, its antlers decorated for whatever occasion was in season. I'm not kidding.

One always ate in the dining room next to the elk. The table was elaborately set with fine china, silver and candles, cloth napkins in special napkin holders decorated with names like "Pearl" and "Harry." Music appropriate to the occasion always played on the stereo. Nancy usually played opera. I was hardly an opera fan when I met them; in fact, it usually made me laugh. But after having been exposed to it at their house, and eventually actually going to the opera, I'm in love with it.

Besides the six-foot elk, there were other stuffed creatures hanging on the walls. They gave me the creeps and I tried to avoid looking at them, but there were also two mallards, an impala, a fox, a deer head, deer antlers, water buffalo horns, a golden pheasant, a common pheasant, a garden-variety male and female pheasant—

and a jackalope. There were also two deer-foot ashtrays, a Canada Goose, and three quail. There were creatures hanging on the walls, no matter where you looked. And two of the windows in that room were covered in crimson red velvet—old theatre curtains, I was told. *But of course, my dear.*

I was at a dinner party there once when one of the guests, Kim, a transvestite and a hooker was trying to convince me that prostitution was a fun gig and that I should try it. *No thank you.* I asked her what she did with her dick when she had a trick. She said, "Oh, my dear. I just tuck it." I found out later that she was transitioning and had given her balls which were preserved in formaldehyde to Ford, one of the models. For a while, those balls were in a jar on the mantel in the living room of Katy and Nancy's house.

Nancy told me that Ford found a family of stuffed Marmots from a defunct Chinese restaurant and gave them to Katy. She said they were very greasy, and she couldn't bear to touch them. *Oh really?* They were kept above an open bookcase in the living room. *Ew.*

All of that stuff was just in the dining room. The cozy living room featured several priceless antiques, including a Chinese processional fan, which hung on the wall, and an antique Chinese chair, made with a thin layer of plaster painted and etched into the wood, which almost no one was ever allowed to sit in. The few people who got to sit there—I wasn't among them—looked like kings or queens, or pharaohs, because of the chair's wide, impressive arms.

For me, this house was so different than what I was used to. My parent's house in Los Angeles was dull as dishwater really. The living room was large with the furniture (vinyl covered couch which stuck to your body if you sat on it and managed not to slide off) crammed against the walls. The room actually made settling noises. It was not conducive to communicating with anyone. Although I do remember one New Year's Eve when my dad had a party and invited therapists and patients. At midnight, the patients were whooping it up, glasses raised, while the therapists had their arms folded tightly across their chests, chain smoking.

So, this house in Noe Valley was like stepping into a movie for me. The move from LA to San Francisco was just that more delicious because of this house.

On the wall closest to the street, which had two large windows on either side, hung a painting of Nancy's called *Venus Anadyomene*, showing the goddess rising from the sea, surrounded by palm trees. Katy had modeled for this, as she did for many of Nancy's paintings. Nancy is really into the classics; she has a reverence for myths and legends, and that comes out in her paintings and poetry. There were seven paintings all around the room and a photograph of Katy.

Under the Chinese fan was a fireplace with a marble mantelpiece that supported two, big, green Chinese vases and two, yellow Chinese dogs on blue stands. All the Chinese stuff, being all the rage in the '70s in San Francisco, had been recently added to the décor. On a little stand were two goldfish in a bowl. There was one color TV set, usually turned to the educational channel and "Mary Hartman, Mary Hartman," the soap-opera that was popular at the time.

There was a large umbrella tree gracing the living room and a cushy couch with down pillows.

And then, there was the beautiful piano, which barely did justice to Katy and Nancy's roommate, Celeste, the woman who often played it, to the pleasure of everyone who heard her. Chopin, Debussy and Beethoven could be heard throughout the house as well as "As Time Goes By" from *Casablanca*. Too often, Earthquake, the parrot, would screech along with her.

The house also featured an extensive collection of antique toys that had come from Nancy's uncle, including a coin bank in the shape of a clown with his tongue stuck out. When you placed a coin on his tongue and pressed a lever, the coin slid back. Deposit made.

The guest bedroom was changed a bit every time a new guest

stayed for a while. After something like two hundred visits, I still couldn't possibly list all the items that filled that house, including live animals, as well as preserved ones. When I first met Katy and Nancy, they had five cats, two dogs and twenty birds. After several years, they were down to two canaries, two peach-faced love birds, a parrot and two pugs. The parrot, Earthquake, was not only unfriendly, but his obnoxious croaking could be heard throughout the house.

Once, someone asked Nancy to "parrot-sit" a bird who had been brought up with a baby. It constantly croaked crying baby sounds.

When a salesman rang the doorbell once, Nancy reluctantly got up off the couch, cigarette in hand, and opened the door. The parrot began screeching, crying baby sounds to the shock of the poor salesman, who said, "Oh, sorry, ma'am. I didn't mean to wake your baby" to which, Nancy growled, "Well, you did!" and slammed the door. She almost liked that bird after that.

The dogs had specific "outdoors" time when they were encouraged to do their outdoor duties, in a fenced-in area Nancy had created to keep the beasts from ruining the garden.

Katy cooked on the kitchen's Wedgewood stove, and Julia Child's cookbook was usually open in the kitchen. She was such a good cook that people hired her for dinner parties. For my birthday, she made Coquilles St. Jacques. I have eaten in some very upscale restaurants here and abroad, but never anything as good as Katy's cooking. Like me, she had grown up on TV dinners, in a home that looked a lot like everyone else's within a large radius and, like most children, she rebelled. But unlike most children, Katy carried her cooking and the décor of her house far beyond rebellion; she made it an art form.

If you didn't know her, Nancy could look formidable, not someone you'd want to mess with. She was tall and thin with a faint scar on her cheek, piercing blue eyes, long fingers and arms.

One time, Katy worked as a cook for one of my dad's month-long workshops in Big Sur. At this workshop, a man from Germany told Nancy, in front of Katy, that she had the fingers of a gynecologist. Katy guffawed and coyly said, "Doctor, doctor", as she wiggled her butt in Nancy's direction.

I, too, took the job of a cook for a month, deciding to take a little break from modeling. One had to plan breakfast, lunch, dinner and appetizers for about 15 people. This wasn't easy, because the closest supermarket was one and a half hours away. If you forgot an ingredient, you were essentially screwed. And, since my dad's property was located on the hazardous Route 1 and accidents were knocking out the power lines at least once a week, the cook had to be prepared to do an impromptu barbeque.

My parents had a hot tub on the property, where people would bask in the sun nearby. At that time—actually, from the time I was 30 to when I was 40—I wore pink, heart-shaped glasses. I had put my lenses under the lounge chair, while I was getting my all-over tan. I needed to drive to Carmel to get the groceries the next hour. When I stood up, I accidentally crunched my glasses with the lounge chair. I couldn't see to drive. So, a woman therapist from the Netherlands, Wendela, offered to drive me into town. Did I white-knuckle the dashboard while she drove like a bat out of hell? Yes. And oh, what fun it was in Safeway trying to read the names of the food items I needed to buy. We obviously didn't die. I'm here to tell the story and to further describe Katy and Nancy's house in Noe Valley.

Katy and Nancy's bedroom was something to behold. It was the kind of place you never wanted to leave. Those two women actually lived out their fantasies. Katy had drawers full of silk costumes, beads, feathers, fantastic old hats and dolls. One day as I sat in their bedroom, I realized their house was like a giant dollhouse.

When I said so, they grinned through a cloud of marijuana, amused at my "realizations."

Katy was the most popular model in San Francisco. Her weight was a big factor in her popularity, but her talents as an artist far surpassed the uniqueness of her voluminous 250-pound body. She not only lived out her fantasies in her life at home, she often carried the settings and props for those fantasies with her, literally, in boxes and sacks when she went out for modeling jobs. She created a fantastic scene when she arrived at an art class and carried her act throughout the entire time, starting with her entrance into the classroom with all of her bags, pillows, and various objects: stuffed armadillos, five-foot butterfly wings, jewels, pillows silken backdrops, elaborate lace fans, rose-pink shoes from the twenties, and giant feathered hats. When she set the scene and put on her partial costume, she did it with all the excitement, charm and allurement that were part of her talent. The first time I drew Katy, I felt like a kid who had just been given a dollar and brought to a candy store.

Once I knew the way to Katy and Nancy's house, I would often end up sleeping there after a job, instead of returning from San Francisco to my Oakland apartment, because it was late, and I was too frazzled to find the Bay Bridge. Honestly, there were a couple of times that I just followed any old car, hoping it would end up going to the Bay Bridge. That never worked. On a few occasions, I found myself in a very sketchy neighborhood in San Francisco. Not fun.

As I got to know Katy and Nancy better, I learned more about how they came to be part of the San Francisco Models Guild. Katy told me she had been an overweight, bored girl whose philosophy in life was "Yes to everything", "More is better" and "Is that all?"!! Katy was probably in her early twenties at the time. She told me she had stood in front of UC Berkeley one day and seen a handsome young man who looked like a Greek god, wearing only a loin cloth. After they did it in the bushes right in front of the school, he told her that he was a model and they needed fat models. He told her she should try out for the San Francisco Models Guild. Like the rest of us, she was scared to death at first, but she went for it and was immediately accepted.

At first, the Guild people told her they were afraid to send her on bookings because of her weight. Some students she modeled for told her they wondered if she could even lift her leg, let alone be graceful with all that weight. The truth is, like any other good model, she knew her body and how it moved, and she knew her limits as well—an important lesson that all models must learn when they start. With her striking grace and style, Katy soon became the most requested model and began to build the Katy Allen legacy.

Once, early in her career, while working at a junior college in Concord, she was wearing her five-foot butterfly wings and a little something covering her crotch. She was then put on a raft in the middle of a pond at the school so the students could draw her there. What the instructor didn't count on was the geese in the pond falling in love with Katy. They chased her around the pond, one goose in particular making such a fuss that soon the entire school knew about it and crowds began to gather. The teacher was running around the pond, yelling, "What are you going to do?" Katy was paddling like crazy to get away from the goose. She finally got off the raft and ran up on the grass. The goose continued to chase her on the grass. The students at Diablo Valley College got the show of their lives that day, watching the humungous artist model wearing nothing but butterfly wings and a little something over her crotch being chased by an enamored goose. Katy finally just ran to her car and took off.

Nancy, I learned, had had an unusual life, growing up with an uncle who had Down's Syndrome and parents who never talked. Her father, who had a strong resemblance to Abraham Lincoln, worked for the railroad. She never had any little kids to play with. Nancy eventually got a scholarship to Stanford, where she studied studio painting. When Katy met her, she was the model secretary for Sacramento State College. Katy convinced Nancy to move to San Francisco and live with her—the beginning of a hot romance that lasted fifteen years.

Katy and her friend Carole opened up a very successful bath boutique called Hanky Panky in San Francisco. One day, about six years after I met them after I had moved to Santa Cruz, I got a call from Nancy saying that Katy and her business partner had been killed in a tragic accident when a truck lost its brakes on a hill. The car was burned beyond recognition. One of the windows was open, however, and Katy and Nancy's pug, Froggy, jumped out of the car and escaped. This news was on the TV and in the S.F. Chronicle for about a week, begging for the return of Froggy. She was returned after about five days. There was a grand memorial for Katy, attended by many models and artists in the community. It was a bittersweet farewell to a San Francisco legend.

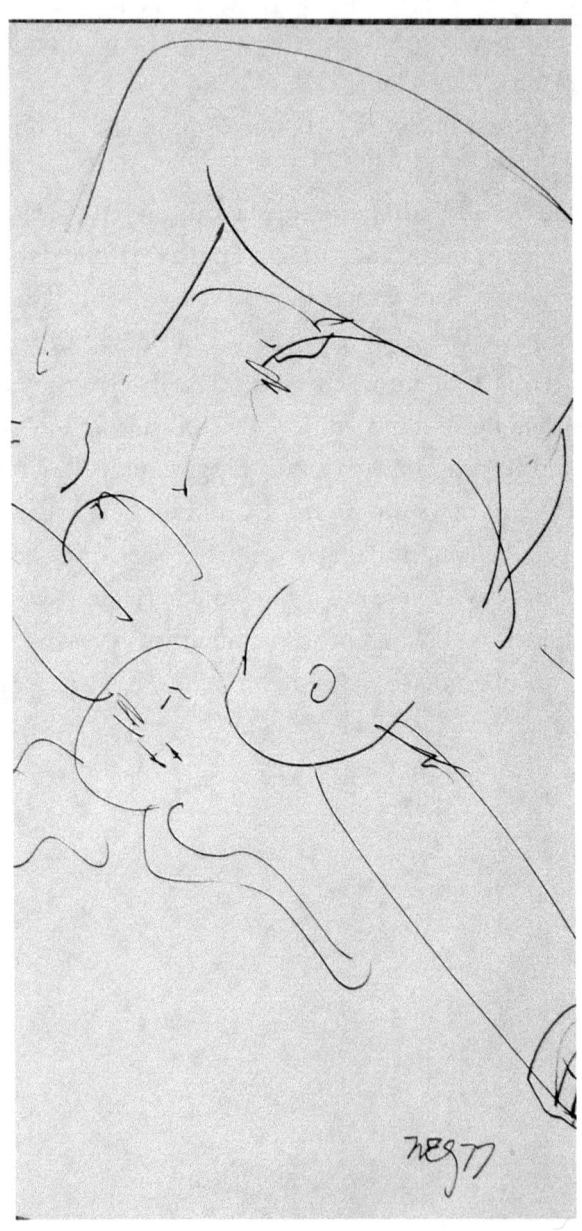

Katy Reclining
Nancy Gotthart, '77

XXXIII

The Redheads

(Margiotta Sisters

&

Other Stories)

I can't really write about the Margiotta sisters, Celeste and Diane, without describing their flowing red tresses and alabaster skin. They were reminiscent of figures in pre-Raphaelite paintings.

CELESTE

ONE OF THE MARGIOTTA SISTERS

Celeste had long, beautiful red hair, pale alabaster skin, a lovely voluptuous body and a baby face with big blue eyes and glasses, which often wore an expression of solemnity. A charming paradox,

Celeste lived permanently in the "honeymoon suite" upstairs at Katy and Nancy's until she moved out. That room, blue and white with a bed so high it was fit for a princess, has witnessed many a romance. Lots o' whoopee had been made in that particular room. Or, as Celeste put it with her innocent face and her big eyes looking as matter-of-fact as possible, "A lot of people have done it in that room." (That was the same room they nursed me in.)

Watching Celeste play the piano was mesmerizing. Just looking at her luxurious, long red hair and the serene look on her face, along with the beautiful music she played was like watching a live painting. After knowing Celeste a little better, it took me and quite a few other people a while to realize that she had an exceptionally dry, sarcastic sense of humor. She spoke very slowly and deliberately, showing very little obvious expression—but her hair was a dead giveaway. The emotional, fiery, explosive, romantic and dramatic personality that went with that red hair was just simmering below the surface, I imagine.

Celeste was an artist as well as a model in the Guild. I modeled with her on occasion. But in the late '70s she had landed what she called a hot job with a printing company and decided to give the "straight" world a try. Being paid for her brains, Celeste dressed in a conservatively feminine style. She wore just about everything I would never wear: rounded necks, soft colors, everything accenting her soft-roundedness. She most often wore her long hair up and tied back. But, if you looked closely, her face revealed a thousand stories. She was always thinking, musing. She was very warm, loving, affectionate, flirtatious, and coy. She often went upstairs to close her door to be private; she needed quiet times and simplicity. When she fell in love, her passion had no limits. When she was hurt, she sunk to the depths of the universe.

DIANE

THE SECOND SISTER

I spoke with Diane recently asking her about modeling memories. She told me a story about when she was sixteen, and her older sister Celeste was nineteen. Celeste had been modeling for the San Francisco Models Guild for a couple of years. I asked Diane if she had ever done a double booking with her. She had. This booking was in an adult education class, somewhere in San Francisco. Diane said that she felt intimidated but was willing to do it. One reason she felt insecure, she said, was because she knew that Celeste was beautiful, and knew she was with long voluptuous breasts, while Diane said she was the tomboy of the two sisters and had a more compact body.

When they got to the booking, Celeste directed Diane to disrobe and sit on the stand facing her. Without being aware of what she was doing, Diane apparently had squeezed her legs together tightly. This was cause for a reprimand from her older sister who advised her that she was to appear relaxed and let her legs spread open. While Diane obeyed her older sister, she felt uncomfortable showing her pubic area to the whole class. The class was small with perhaps 16 students, who were seemingly oblivious to Diane's inner turmoil. During the breaks, Diane recalled following close behind her sister or the teacher and not looking at the drawings that the students did.

A few years later, she too started modeling for the Guild. One of her triumphs was when she modeled for a man who had a studio on Geary Blvd. and was quite well-known, Arnold Schoenberg. She had heard that he paid well too.

This was during a time when she was making costumes in high school and had saved one of them. It was a Renaissance inspired dress in red velvet. She brought a beautiful dress to his studio, and he did large pastel drawings of her in that dress. Diane said, "He made me look beautiful."

He told her later that he had sold a drawing, or two, and made quite a bit of money. When she asked him if she could have part of it, he declined, saying he had already paid her. What happened later when her sister Celeste picked her up from his studio was a big verbal dressing down. It seemed, according to Diane, that Celeste was pissed off that Diane got that booking instead of her.

Diane recounted another story about a class she took at Humboldt State College. She said that the teacher asked all the students to disrobe and put masks on, covering their eyes. The teacher wanted the students to have the experience of doing what is called blind contour drawings of one another. So, they paired off and with a pencil in one hand, they reached out with the other, feeling the shape of the student who was their partner as they drew them. She said everyone was willing to do this, and the drawings were quite wonderful. She saved one of them for years.

She told me another story that one doesn't hear every day. I've been laughing about this one for days. For several years in a building in Santa Cruz called The Art League, there was a life-sized wax sculpture of *The Last Supper*. It was placed on a stage in a room that had seats arranged as if in a church. During an unusual, and particularly stormy evening, the teacher had the model climb up and pose on the stage in front of the sculpture. The storm began to rage, replete with thunder and lightning. This was disconcerting enough in Santa Cruz, as we were unused to this kind of weather, but having it flash over *The Last Supper* was too much for the students in the class. One by one, they picked up their supplies and fled the building. *Maybe they thought God was angry?* The instructor was left alone with the model and *The Last Supper*.

I remember this exhibit only too well, having been kicked out many years before. My roommate and I got stoned and decided to check it out. When one walked in, there was a box in which one was encouraged to donate what they could. When we walked in, we were greeted by two rather prim looking church ladies; their lips were tight in straight lines. We were decidedly disapproved of. As we entered the dimly lit room, there was a scratchy tape playing about *The Last Supper*. We noticed that only Judas had dark brown hair and a hook nose, all the rest being blonde, of course. This caused our stoned selves to burst into uncontrollable giggles. The ladies descended upon us and ordered us to leave. We were only too glad to do so.

Thinking back to the '70s, the Margiotta sisters were a big part of my modeling memories. I feel lucky that I'm still in touch with them. Some of the models in the poster have passed and others I've tried unsuccessfully to find.

XXXIV

Who Would Do That?

There was a woman in San Francisco who was very interesting to work for. She was quite elderly, clever, and liberal, a well-educated gentlewoman who liked to draw models doing simple poses. She was also quite well to do. Her house was lovely with a beautiful garden outside, greeting you as you entered. Inside, the house was filled with art objects; the likes of which one might see in a museum. She was an accomplished painter with her paintings adorning her drawing studio. It was difficult for her to walk—I was always afraid she might fall—but she was resigned to the tribulations of getting old. I loved working for her because she was so elegant. Always polite, she would occasionally make a little witty comment, which endeared me to her even more. I did, however, have a hard time working for her because she liked the more simple, natural kind of poses. My repertoire didn't include many of this type.

Once, for a change, I thought I would really impress her with what I thought was my most beautiful pose. So, there I was, thinking that I looked beautiful, indeed. When I looked up at her, she had a smile on her face and couldn't contain her laughter. When she regained her composure, she said, "Why, who in the world would ever do that?"

So much for my pose. My thought was "*I would. I just did it.*"

I soon had to stop working for her because if she liked you, she'd hire you every week. Then, driving over there, I would be freaking out, thinking, *What the hell new kind of simple pose could I possibly do sitting in that same chair?*

I mean the body can only do so much with limited circumstances.

XXXV

Stars and Stripes Knee Socks

So, what happens when a drawing, painting or sculpture of you is recognizable as you, and it's displayed in public?

Well, I once had a guy I dated in high school tell me he was appalled when he saw a drawing of me in a gallery somewhere. *Appalled? Tsk! Tsk!*

Sometimes, finding a drawing, print or painting can be very unexpectedly useful! Get this.. sometime in the late '70s, my BFF Laverne and her friend Cynthia had planned a day trip to the city (that's San Francisco). They had to leave early (they lived in Seaside) to get there with enough time to go to Chinatown to eat dim sum at Cynthia's favorite restaurant, which reminded her of her childhood in Hong Kong.

After breakfast, they walked around and checked out all the open-air markets with live fish and other seafood. They passed by shop windows filled with roasted ducks and chickens hanging by their necks.

They headed down to Pier 39, playing tourists, enjoying shopping, checking out the sea lions barking and street performers. In one art gallery, they came across a print of me in my stars-and-stripes, knee high socks.

They were stoked to see it, recognizing me. Of course, it was way too expensive for either of them, even if they pooled their money together, so they just left it there and couldn't wait to get back and tell me all about it.

After a scrumptious dinner at Fisherman's Wharf (huge sourdough bowls filled with clam chowder), they headed to the car only to find the engine wouldn't turn over. They figured it was the battery, so they walked over to a phone booth and called AAA. The truck came out and said it wasn't the battery. Someone had stolen the starter! At this point it was around 7 p.m. on a Saturday and the mechanic from AAA said all the shops were closed.

They went back to the phone booth, where Laverne called her husband who wasn't home. Then, she called me to see if I could give her the phone number for Katy and Nancy, to see if they could spend the night at their house. However, much to their dismay, I wasn't home either. Laverne couldn't remember Katy or Nancy's last names, so the phone book wouldn't have been much use. But, they remembered that the print of me was signed by the artist and because of tourism the gallery was luckily still open. They found the print, wrote down the artist's name, went back to the phone booth, looked up his name, called him and he answered! She told him the story, and then he gladly gave them the phone number for the San Francisco Model's Guild, which happened to be Katy and Nancy's number. And yes, they answered!

Laverne doesn't remember if she and Cynthia took a taxi to Katy and Nancy's, or if they came and got them, but they were given the royal treatment, including a breakfast the next day with chocolate croissants and huge mugs of really strong coffee.

They went to the auto shop, bought a starter for Cynthia's turquoise Mazda, called AAA again, and soon were off and running!

Laverne said now she wished she had bought the print!

XXXVI

Artists in the Bay Area

Norbert Schlaus

There was a man who lived in Oakland, whose art resembled that of Hieronymus Bosch. I was warned that although he was innocuous, it was difficult to work for him. My attitude was, *how bad could it be?*

The first time I went to work for him, I walked up the steps of an older apartment building and knocked on the door. I heard footsteps in the background, but no one came to the door. I knocked yet again. Soon, the door opened, and I saw a tall, thin man with round wireframe glasses, pale skin that looked like he'd never seen the sun, a flannel jacket that was frayed at the sleeves and looked two sizes two big, and khaki pants that were tied together with string. He opened the door wider, did an odd little bow, and motioned for me to come inside. With his right arm, he gestured toward a door and said in almost a whisper, "You can change in there." I noticed right away that he barely moved his lips and didn't smile.

"Would you like a twenty-minute pose?" I ventured as I came out in my robe.

He nodded, sat down opposite me, and proceeded to draw.

Several times, he offered me a glass of water, which I declined. I could hear someone in the bedroom. He noticed this and said simply,

"That's my mother. Don't mind her. She's very old and can't hear or see very well."

He most often didn't speak, but over the course of working for him for three or four weeks in a row, I managed to hear part of his story.

I was told he had come with his mother from Germany, soon after the war, and for who knows what reason, they ended up in Oakland. I don't know how he got the apartment, but he said he was afraid to leave his mother alone, and when they first arrived, neither of them spoke English. They stayed in the apartment for several days without eating. He knew he had to venture out into this strange city in this strange new country and get some food and something to drink, so he walked outside to look for a store. He wandered around and got lost. A policeman saw him and started questioning him. He couldn't speak English, started to tremble and basically freak out by being interrogated by a police officer. The officer thought he was drunk and took him to jail. He was terrified in jail and worried about his mother. No one spoke German. He thought they must have thought he was delirious.

In the morning, they let him go. It took him a while to find his apartment again, but once inside, he found his mother was okay, albeit worried. He went out again, bought groceries for a week and almost never left the apartment again. He only left to buy groceries. I never found out how he got the money for them. After being there for a while, he did venture out on occasion and passed an art gallery.

He decided to show the owner his drawings. They were quite good, and he sold enough to pay for rent, food, and models.

I don't remember what I said, but once I made him smile. When he smiled, I noticed he had what looked like braces on his teeth. When I asked him about that, he got quiet. He told me he had no real teeth. I hesitated but asked him if he had been in the camps in Germany. He nodded. I then asked him if it was painful. He got quiet again and then said, "You get used to it. The pain goes away."

The last time I worked for him, he told me that the art dealer had offered to give him a show, but he had refused. He told the dealer that he could sell his work, but that there was no way he would go to an opening.

When I asked him about that, he looked at me and said, "I can't be around people."

I never knew what happened to him or his mother. I found it too emotionally painful to work for him. His pain and neediness overwhelmed me.

When I told him I could no longer work for him, he just nodded and said,

"Thank you for your time."

He gave me a copy of an etching, which I saved. While writing this memoir, someone suggested I Google him. I had no idea he was so famous!

Etching
Norbert Schlaus

XXXVII

Meeting Franklin Williams

One of the best parts about modeling has been meeting pretty famous painters and sculptors. I often learned a lot. For example, I got to meet Franklin Williams (F.W.), because one morning Katy woke me up at 6 a.m. and asked if I could take her bookings at the Art Institute for the day. She had been up all night, coughing with bronchitis. I told her I would, and she, being forever grateful, made me breakfast and packed me four hot costumes. I didn't relish the thought of facing a teacher and students who were expecting the famous Katy Allen, but I had never worked for F.W., and I thought it might be fun to work for someone new. The only thing I knew about him previously to this meeting was that he had tied up one of the models in the San Francisco Models Guild with her permission. When I later asked him about this, he added a few more bondage/sculptural-type stories. One day, he wrapped a model up in gobs of toilet paper and then spent a good half hour spreading peanut butter on the toilet paper. "Didn't that look like shit?" asked I.

"Yes," he replied with a grin.

I showed up and told him that Katy had given me the booking. He smiled at me and told me that he had made a mistake and really didn't need a model, but that if I wanted, I could come with his class. He told me that he was driving up the coast in his Porsche. I immediately said, "Yes." He then said "Oh, we're really not doing that. We're actually flying down to L.A. for the weekend." I agree to that one too. *I don't think he expected me to agree to everything he said.* Then, he told me the truth. They were all going to see his teaching assistant's studio and discuss art and eat. I could come along and get paid for it. So, off I went, collecting stories from F.W. in the car on the way to the studio.

The studio was in a warehouse upstairs, somewhere near Market Street, downtown. It had high ceilings, lots of space and light, and wasn't too cozy. Once we got inside, we were given pillows to sit on. Those kinds of places are always creatively decorated inside with makeshift living spaces, suggesting the poor, starving artist's décor, and always freezing. There was one patch of sunlight on the floor about two inches square. All 6'2", or so, of F.W. immediately placed himself on the square of sunlight and bolted down on his heels. He started making crowing movements and noises, as if he was a rooster. He was outrageous.

During the morning, "pearls of wisdom" were dropping from his mouth about the meaning of art. He said it didn't fill in all the cracks, and if you thought it would, you would be very frustrated. I guess, it was the last class, and he was exchanging feedback with his students. There were about eight women and one Catholic priest there. At lunchtime, all of a sudden, lots of food and wine appeared and our conversation soon became quite personal. We talked about love and men and sex. After a while, I asked the priest if these were the kinds of things he heard in confession. He replied, "Never this interesting."

Then, the teaching assistant told a story about when she was seven years old, she went to confession and hadn't committed any of the sins. She was standing in line and freaking out, thinking that she had to have committed something, so since she didn't know what adultery was, she said, "Forgive me, Father, for I have sinned. I have committed adultery five times." She heard the priest howl with laughter.

Then, the priest told us a story about how a little boy of five had told him that he had committed adultery. He asked this little boy what that meant, and he replied, "Peeing on the outside of the church building." Later that afternoon, after hearing a lot of complaints about men, F.W. offered the observation that pleasing a woman was really *so* very simple, and if men would only realize this, they would find it very easy. All you had to do was give her a flower or tell her she's beautiful or appreciate her in some way, every day. I told him that his wife was very lucky. He said, "I'm very lucky too. I've been married 15 years to the same woman and have beautiful children. The other way is too easy—to just leave."

His artwork has a lot of sewn things in it, and he said at openings people are disappointed that he is a man. In his studio, he has a sewing machine and weights. He talked about the athlete and the artist as being very similar. He said he works out in the early morning, and then paints or sculpts or whatever for hours, and then, to let off steam, and to stretch his body out, he does intense physical exercise again for a few hours.

The whole day for me was a treat. If this hadn't had been the last day of class, I probably would have never gotten so close, so fast to all these people. I came home and told Katy. She was very jealous, but her bronchitis had gotten a lot better.

ABSTRACT EXPRESSIONISM

Franklin Williams told me that he often posed with the model he had hired. Once, during a lecture on abstract expressionism, he tied one end of a string around his middle finger and the other end of the string around the middle finger of the model, and then he continued to wrap more and more thread around both of them until they were tied together near the wall. He continued to lecture, quietly asking a student to get up and wrap big pieces of nylon around him and the model and to staple them to the wall.

ON THE WALL

Another F.W. wall story: He had a model stand against the wall and kept putting big pieces of billboard paper over her, while stapling the paper to the wall. Then while he was lecturing on abstract expressionism, he would tear a piece of the billboard paper off the model and have the students draw what they could see of the billboard paper and the model behind it. He continued to tear pieces until they could see most of the model. Depending on the model, it must have been fun. This reminded me of when I worked for Diebenkorn in L.A., and he had me inside of cardboard boxes. I never really got to be seen at all. That was not fun.

HANGING DOWN

Another time, F. W. built a small frame of 2x6s for the model in the rafters above the class. He had her hang there, looking down at the students, while they were lying on their backs and drawing on little pieces of paper. They could see only parts of the body and parts of the structure.

In thinking about why I even liked modeling, I realized it was the spontaneity of it that appealed to me. When I moved up to the Bay Area, it was a time of self-reflection. Modeling is all about being spontaneous. I feel good when that happens and bored with repetition. I have a strong saboteur inside of me, warning me about consequences. I think, this is why modeling was so appealing. It's a job where there are many new locations, new faces, new poses. One can be asked to look like a Matisse painting or to bring unusual props. The whole unknown quality is what I like about it. I even enjoyed being a Kelly Girl, years ago, because I would go to different jobs all the time and never had the opportunity to get bored. Living in Oakland, Berkeley or San Francisco had it all there, right in front of me.

My significant other at the time wanted us to live somewhere in between his parents and my parents. His parents lived in the East Bay, while mine were in Big Sur. His grandparents wanted us to get married, so we went to Monterey and did that on the judge's lunch hour, because he had forgotten about us in Castroville and we had to find him in Pacific Grove.

So, in a way, moving to Monterey, California, after the Bay Area did provide a good space for asking myself: *What had I been doing and where was I going?* When I lived in Monterey in 1975, it was easier to get bored and be forced to soulsearch. Although, it was known to be an art center of sorts, Monterey had very few modeling jobs. The pay was low; the level of interest also seemed low, and despite a few exceptions now and then, there were some very stodgy ideas about life drawing permeating the atmosphere.

I used to get insulted when someone would say, "What else do you do?" as if being an artist model wasn't enough for anyone to do. There are some models who have done it for 25-30 years. That sounds very romantic. There was one model in Los Angeles who had been modeling most of her life. She was a queen— regal, lovely. When I left, she was still modeling, in between going to peace marches and rallies. She had grey hair and a lovely posture and grace. You could just tell she had done it for years. And then, of course, in San Francisco, there was Flo Allen. I admire the legends of artist modeling, and their commitment to the art. This kind of commitment is something that I fear. However, if I ever finish this book, that will be a promise to myself.

Of course, I didn't realize then, that unless I got total enjoyment out of being a model and was satisfied with earning $200-$300 a month, then it wasn't enough. Yet, living in the Bay Area provided enough entertainment that I could probably have continued modeling and being satisfied being poor. But at that time, I was also very attracted to travel. I was always, and am still, interested in others who are different than I am. So, if I wanted to travel, I was going to have to find another job, so I could earn the money to do it.

XXXVIII

Monkey Shit

There was a man in San Francisco who had a studio in a warehouse. He was a very spaced-out little guy with scraggly hair and a tendency to shuffle around. He also had a thing for animals—unusual animals. He had one of those dogs that look like sharks. Actually, it was a very sweet dog. It just looked scary. It was always waiting at the top of the stairs, whenever I got there. My heart would stop for a second, and then I would remember that it was nice. He also had a monkey, which would perch atop my head while I modeled. I was always worried that it would shit, which it would. He also had one silver pheasant and its mate, a trumpeter bird, a parakeet, and a parrot. I think each of his birds came to a sad ending, getting caught in the rafters and flying out his windows. A girlfriend of mine went out with him once and said he had playboy foldouts pasted on the roof of his Volkswagen. Last I heard, he joined the Hells Angels.

XXXIX

Shit that Happens

Hold Still

One day in Monterey, I was modeling for a beginning art class. They were working on portraits. The teacher actually asked, "Can you hold a facial expression for three minutes?" *No.* Then, she said, "How about 1 minute?" *No.* Then, "30 seconds?" I really didn't think I could do it, but *I'll try.* This seemed not only ridiculous, but uninspiring at best. I suggested that I stand up on a bench, so the whole class could see me. On that bench, I suddenly felt naked. Well, I was. But they were only drawing my face, so I thought I should have my robe on at least. However, it was too late. I was already up on the bench. Standing naked on a bench while trying to hold a facial expression for 30 seconds, I felt quite ridiculous. I hemmed and hawed for a minute, while the teacher started walking around asking if anyone knew an actor or a mime. Well, that got me. I was an actor for Christ's sake. I hadn't been asked to emote for several years, but I did have the training. All this time I was questioning myself as to whether even an actor or a mime would have to hold a facial expression for 30 seconds. It may not sound long to you but try it sometime.

After much ado, I finally imagined "fear" and did a rather bland facial portrayal of fear. Then, I did a pout. (That was easy.) Then, I freaked out a little while longer, while the teacher kept repeating the need for an actor or a mime. I then made the gross mistake of trying "joy" for 30 seconds. The teacher was kind enough to say that this one would be short. I felt stumped yet again when the teacher said, "Do fear, Helene." Well, fuck if I was going to tell her I already did "fear." My ego was hurting. I faintly repeated, "Fear? Oh, yes...fear." And then, I did "fear." I got down from the bench, hearing her repeat the need for an actor or a mime for the final time. I went home feeling nonplussed and asked my then husband what he would do for a 30-second expression. Well, he did one by scrunching up his face and going cross-eyed. This cracked both of us up. Pretty soon we both almost pissed ourselves laughing. Since he reminded me of a cross between Robin Williams and Robert Redford, that expression seemed to me to be his essential core.

The next day I asked a girlfriend of mine, who tended to be rather condescending, to do one. She did a typically patronizing face, while saying to me, "Helene, I could hold this for five minutes." So...Ah so. I thought I had a theory. Whatever face people picked for their first expression was the core of their personality, but, thanks to my sister Josefa, who did a totally ridiculous kind of munchkin-turtlebeaver face, my theory was unfounded. One friend, who had been reading a lot of writings by psychoanalyst Wilhelm Reich, suggested that it might be the mask that people used most often. Whatever, it was a ridiculous suggestion for an art teacher to give a model.

XL

Some Hazards of Being a Model

Modeling is wonderful, but some aspects are less than desirable. For instance, one thing all artist models have experienced is being too cold. Some artists laugh and call it a hazard of the profession. Ha. Ha. The thing is that it's hard to draw when you're too warm, apparently, and hard to model when you're too cold. When I'm too cold, I find myself taking very closed-in poses, trying to keep myself warm, or I envision myself eating a hot bowl of chili. This works, as long as I can keep the fantasy up, about 5 minutes. Or, I take deep breaths. I often ask them to turn up the heat or get me a heater. Sometimes, I need two heaters, one for the front and one for the back.

A model need not disrobe if "adequate heat" is not provided or if there is not enough privacy, according to the Guild's guidelines.

Once, in a warehouse in San Francisco, the artists were wearing their coats and gloves. I could see their breath. They stood there, expecting me to disrobe. *Um, no.*

Along with being cold, having a cold or a cough can be very embarrassing on the model's stand. Sitting up there with a box of Kleenex by your side and silently choking is never much fun. It does seem to make them realize you're a person, but they also sometimes seem to resent that fact as well: *How dare that model cough when I'm drawing her mouth? She's paid to sit still.* One of the worst feelings is knowing that within a second, or two, you will no longer be able to control your cough, and you'll have to break the pose, maybe even ask for a glass of water. Or, your nose will start dripping and you don't have a tissue, so you keep wiping it off with your hand, while trying to maintain the pose and the mood. Usually, though, there is some kind Nurse Barton type in the class who will rush off and get you the drink of water or the lozenge or the tissue, whatever you need.

And then, there's the experience of watching some slimy guy slither into class, trying to appear innocuous, while he gaped at the "naked" person in the room. His mouth was open, cheeks burning red. This is, at the very least, disconcerting. Don't tell me he's interested in art.

A lot of people think that artist models and photographers' models are one in the same. Not true! Posing for them is not the same thing at all. Not all of them, but a lot of photographers are interested in things like shaved armpits, no zits, shaved legs on women, glamor. The whole creative process takes a lot less time on the part of the model and it is made by a machine. Now, many photographers are not like this, but I did a lot more scrutinizing before I would work for a photographer. I worried about being misused or abused. The San Francisco Models Guild had a big rule about no cameras allowed in the room. If someone wanted to take a photo, they had to ask the model. The few times I agreed to let a photographer take my picture, I was promised money or prints and never received either. This gave me mixed emotions about photographers. In general, they didn't have very good reputations among artist models.

As far as hazards are concerned, a story from Los Angeles comes to mind:

One of the teachers, maybe Jean Barlow, asked me to come dressed as a Max Beckmann painting. Of course, I had to look that up. I painted one side of my face red and the other blue, got in my red VW Bug and sped off to the class. Unfortunately, a cop pulled me over. The look on his face was almost worth the whole ticket.

"You were going 15 miles past the speed limit."

"I was? Oh, sorry, Officer. I, uh, well, as you can see, I'm on my way to model for a painting class at Santa Monica City College."

"Uh huh," He mumbled, as he wrote out the big fat ticket.

"*Asshole*," I thought, "he could at least ask me about the artist." He didn't.

XLI

Taking an Unauthorized Booking

Every job through the San Francisco Models Guild was checked out ahead of time. Once in a great while, I made the mistake of taking a job that wasn't through the Guild. A model friend of mine called Tiny Merille got me one of these jobs. Tiny Merrille was a kick. Once, she came to visit me from NYC in the dead of winter. She rode on the back of a motorcycle cross-country. She was badass. She was also one of the few people who had a tattoo, long before they became popular. She had a little green cabbage on her right buttock: *Mon petit chou chou* (a French endearment: my little cabbage). The job she got me was in the Mission District in San Francisco in a warehouse. She told me that the guy in charge of the class had some connection with the San Francisco Art Institute, so I thought it was safe. Not really.

When I walked in, there were about 30 Samoan teenage boys—no girls—drinking beer, smoking dope and listening to the boombox provided by the teacher, a cool looking Chicano dude. He informed me that these kids were from Samoa and they were mellow. They had all been provided with drawing paper and pencils. They smiled at me and asked me if I wanted a toke or two. No, thank you. I was already pretty scared; all I needed was to have reefer paranoia. The thing about Samoans is they are very big physically. I felt myself getting the preliminaries of a migraine. This was not a good sign.

About 15 minutes after I arrived, another woman showed up. She too was a model. I was at once relieved. She looked surprised to see me there, but we disrobed and started working together. The kids actually drew for the first hour or so, but they kept drinking more beer and smoking more dope. Pretty soon, the pencils dropped, and they were just flat out leering at us. I wasn't sure if they had ever drawn the nude before. I couldn't look any of them in the face. I looked through them and tried to pretend I felt at ease. My headache was intensifying to the point of nausea. When the time was up, Mr. Suave-Hippy-Cool-Man-Groovy-Guy said he couldn't pay me that night, but not to worry, because he'd get me the money. He had made a mistake and double-booked us. *Sure.* It took a lot of hassle and time to finally get my money some months later. The whole time he was acting like I was a totally uncool chick who only cared about money. Like, *mellow out.* Mellow out, my ass, buddy!

XLII

Bugs

I couldn't write a book about the traumas models have to deal with without mentioning bugs. I mean, there I am sitting still, settling into a 20-minute pose, and along comes a fly or a gnat or any creepy-crawly, and all of a sudden, I feel like I'm being tickled somewhere. First, I try to ignore it. *Will it go away?* Then, I try to concentrate on another part of my body, but sooner or later, it becomes unbearable, and I have to break the pose to scratch or swat it away. Anywhere a bug crawls is disconcerting, some places more than others.

Yoko Ono made a movie in which a fly slowly crawls across a woman's body and she just lies there and takes it. The whole time all you hear is the buzzing of the fly. The movie was a social comment about women, but I can relate to that as an artist model as well. The feeling of vulnerability is overpowering.

XLIII

Dogs

A long time ago, I took a drawing class. The teacher was from London. He dressed impeccably, spoke softly and was thoroughly exasperated with me because I was the only person in the class who couldn't see "perspective." I still have difficulties with that. What he didn't know was that I had covered myself up entirely with a parasol on a previous modeling job. You should see me park my car.

There was a rather loud, sexy woman in our class who wore really short, low-cut dresses, black stockings, gobs of makeup and perfume. She used to delight in literally backing that teacher up against the wall with her bosom. He would just blush and keep walking backwards until she had him pinned to the wall.

I heard a story from a model who worked for this teacher once. That particular morning, it would have been a good idea for her to have taken a shower before going to the class, considering her activities prior to leaving. She put on her robe when she got to the classroom, sat on a stool and waited for him to finish the lecture he was giving in a different part of the room. Someone had brought their dog, and within minutes this dog was humping the stool she was sitting on. She couldn't get it to stop. First, she tried being nice. "Down, dog....down dog." Then she tried being stern.

"Get down, you bad dog...get the fuck away from that stool...Go sit down, you stupid dog."

Luckily, most of the class was still paying attention to the lecture on the other side of the room. The teacher soon noticed and elongated his lecture for her benefit, but the dog would not be deterred. The model noticed one of the students smiling at the dog and asked her if it belonged to her. The student said, "Yes. Oh, don't mind him. He's a peenie licker from way back."

The model finally persuaded her to put her "peenie licker" out in the hall until class was over. Personal hygiene is rather important in this business.

XLIV

Other Hazards

Another time, a well-meaning (I suppose) art student asked me to please stop breathing.

A friend of mine was asked if he would consent to copulate with a skeleton. Guess what his answer was?

The friend who turned me on to modeling in the first place was literally strapped to the wall spread-eagle for an anatomy class, while the teacher employed wooden pointers for "muscle identification."

Another model was subjected to an instructor running his hand between her legs while explaining "negative space." *Uh huh.*

One afternoon I had a job at a building in Golden Gate Park in San Francisco. The room I was in was quite large, with very high ceilings and lots of windows. The windows were covered with paper and taped up to insure privacy. I was doing a standing pose with a partial costume, consisting of a wide-brimmed hat covered with red feathers and black high-heeled shoes. There were a lot of little kids playing outside. Somehow, in the midst of the pose, a young kid about 10 years old wandered in and stopped dead in his tracks when he saw me. He kind of freaked out and started yelling obscenities at me. The teacher and I thought nothing of it, and he was politely asked to leave.

Unfortunately, we didn't realize what seeing a nude model would do to a kid that age. Within minutes the walls of the building were being scaled by about twenty young boys. They were like insane praying mantises, climbing the walls, peering in through the windows. The language coming out of their mouths blew my mind. Especially since most of it was directed at me. The class had to be stopped. Everyone had to leave. The older students in the class were particularly upset. I was afraid to walk to my car without an escort. Needless to say, a screen was promptly erected the next day and the door was kept locked after the class started. That building mysteriously burned down several years later.

XLV

Fetishes

In San Francisco I worked for adult school classes. One incident from that time sticks out in my mind. There was an older Asian gentleman who insisted that I wear my hair up. I didn't like to do that, but I acquiesced. He would get very upset if he couldn't see the nape of my neck, which I surmised was considered an erotic part of the body in the culture he came from. In that class, there were about twenty or so students. About a third of them preferred me to look more classical with my hair up and my glasses off. The other two thirds of them were younger and didn't have any such preferences, as long as they had a model. They would even draw a model clothed and be grateful for it. It got to the point with this irritating man that whenever I saw him, I would immediately put my hair up begrudgingly.

He normally came early, but one day, he wasn't there when class started. I was very relieved and happily started doing the usual 5-minute, warm-up poses. During the second one, out of the corner of my eye, I saw him come barreling into the room. My first thought was *Uh oh*. My second thought was *Fuck you*. I mean, after all, he was late, and I was in the middle of a pose. I thought to myself, *I'll just put my hair up during my first break in about ten minutes*. The little man took one look at me, stormed over to a chair, gritting his teeth, veins popping out in his neck, and began to jump up and down, screaming at me. He looked like a five-year-old having a temper tantrum. I felt my face turning red. I was embarrassed and angry. I wanted to kick his little head right off. I yelled back at him, pointing to the rubber band around my wrist, and said, "This is for you." Meaning that I would tie my hair up with the rubber band in case he came to class.

The thing about this annoying little man was that he never asked me personally to tie my hair up. He would always ask the teacher to tell me I had to. I found this chickenshit. So, after this outburst I had a difficult time enjoying myself for the rest of the evening. The students in the class were consoling me on my breaks, saying he was bonkers and not to take it personally. I told the teacher that she should have supported me and asked the man to leave. This teacher, however, was the kind of person with a heart of gold and could never ask a student to leave. It was her livelihood, after all. She got rehired according to how many students were in attendance. So, out of kindness to the student and for the sake of her pocketbook, she wasn't able to support me.

I reported this incident at the next San Francisco Models Guild meeting. They came to my rescue by writing a letter to Adult Ed, saying that even though the teacher was being kind to her student and not wanting to cause a disruption, a model didn't have to be insulted like that. It is the instructor's job to reprimand the person who is responsible for the disturbance. The letter also said, if it happened again with the same student, he/she should be asked to leave.

The Models Guild has been known to blackball teachers who have been unduly rude to models. We would be allowed to work for them, if we chose to, but we would not be penalized if we walked out on them either.

XLVI

Artistic Whims

Harness

Quite a few years ago, there was a teacher at the Art Institute of San Francisco who decided to design a harness for the model and to hoist her up in the air, swing her to and fro and have the students draw her. However, he ran into technical difficulties. The harness didn't quite conform to the poor model's body, and there she was, up in the air, screaming in pain because the harness was too tight while the students were drawing her, not understanding. Meanwhile, the teacher was desperately trying to get her down. The apparatus had stuck, and she continued to scream while the students continued to draw. After fifteen minutes, he managed to get her down. She put her clothes on and left.

XLVII

Fake Zits

    In Los Angeles on the first day of class, Les Biller brought with him several packages of fake zits that he had bought at the dime store. He put these on his face, boils included, and proceeded to give a slide lecture to his students who were staring at his face. During the course of the lecture, he would take the zits and boils off one by one and put them in his pocket.

XLVIII

Fetishes in Berkeley

There was an old, dark, creepy two-story house on a typical street in Berkeley in which there lived a polite, older gentleman who drew a nude once a week. He was also known for throwing parties once in a while and inviting as many models as would come.

This is how an evening at his house began: The house looked dark. You'd walk up and as you did, you'd see a curtain open just a crack. You'd then knock on the door. It immediately opened, and there he was, standing tall with a smile on his face, bowing politely as he handed you a flower from his garden and said, "How beautiful to see you, my dear." You'd then walk inside and see piles and piles of girlie magazines stacked up on the floor, girlie statues, swords, curtains held up on a high ledge with books instead of curtain rods, low lights, old furniture that looked like it hadn't been dusted in years, and old bookcases full of hard to distinguish images on the covers of hardback books.

Then, you'd follow him up a long, narrow, creaky staircase to the room where he drew the models. He usually sat very close to the model and preferred poses where she was prone with her feet close to him. Before the session started, I usually rushed off to the bathroom for the last few moments of sanity, as I changed into my robe and came out to greet him. During the model's first break, he asked you if you wanted some chocolates. (Is the Pope Catholic?) At the next break, you'd get offered a glass of sherry. Next break, cigarettes, and then the offers started all over again. During these times, he loved to talk about car problems and what particular cut of steaks he was going to serve you. This was said with the same glint in his eye as when he offered you chocolates. I'm glad that's all we ever talked to him about.

At the end of the evening, he politely walked you down the stairs, paid you more than the going rate, bowed as he smiled and said, "goodbye." and that he hoped to see you again soon. He also asked if you would ever be available to come to one of his parties. I personally have never been to one, but this is what I was told: He would buy a lot of steaks and the models cooked those and something else. Everyone got a little tipsy. The models enjoyed teasing him and acting very silly. He got a few little pinches in here and there, but mainly he was a voyeur, which he was the first to admit. Once, one of the models disrobed and danced on his dining room table. That may have been the highlight of his life. He always asked the models if they would do that again at one of his parties. They teased him and asked him to do it himself.

This tickled him, and giggling, he'd say, "My dear, I'm a voyeur!" All in all, the women who attended his parties had a wonderful time, loved him, and thought of him as a harmless, lovely gentleman.

XLIX

Unfortunate Bodily Functions

There are a few delicate bodily functions that most people who draw or paint models don't think about. One of them is flatulence. It's pretty uncomfortable, to say the least, if you're up on the stand and you know you have to fart. I can guarantee models have perfected talented sphincter muscles. It's possible and preferable to control one's sphincter so that no one is aware if the model has farted. The model is probably hoping that the artists suspect someone else in the room, especially if they have kept a straight and ever-so-innocent-looking face. If you have the unfortunate experience of it suddenly coming out loud and clear, the question is whether to openly say, "Excuse me," thereby admitting to this heinous act and possibly breaking the concentration of the artists who may not have heard it, or just pretending it didn't happen. There is always the option of staring at someone, as if they were the culprit, but that's not nice.

Speaking of emissions, there's another thing that models have to contend with. It's kind of gross, but there you have it. If you're a guy and you get the clap and don't know it yet, it can be very embarrassing if you find out you have it while you're on the model's stand. This has happened, I'm told. Or, if you're a woman and you suddenly get your period on the stand, that can also be a very unfortunate experience, if not uncommon. The worst part is the decision you have to make: whether to acknowledge what has happened and leave the stand or pretend you don't notice it and hope no one else does. These intimate facts of life are just so much more intense during a class, when you just so happen to be nude with 30 or so people drawing or painting you, and you are the center of attention.

At the Models Guild meeting at the beginning of each year, the president has to remind the female models to tuck their tampon strings up while modeling. There is too much of a distraction if you are in a standing pose and the students are watching your string hang or sway in the breeze. I honestly heard of a woman in Los Angeles who refused to tuck the string up and painted it with dark brown shoe polish instead. Gross. Different strokes. Some women will cut the strings short—a better solution, in my humble opinion.

L

Interviews with Infamous Artist Models from the '70s

Toni Tandalayo

THE FATAL FALL

One of the most flamboyant and fun models in the Guild was Toni Tandalayo, whose last name was given to her by a cousin, inspired by a seductive middle eastern character in a 1942 movie. Toni said her heritage was part Native American, and people often took her for a full-blooded Indian, especially when she let her hair down and wore a headband. An ordained minister, as well as a model, she sometimes signed her letters as "the beautiful, mystical, mysterious practitioner, model, singer, dancer, actress and intriguin' in all mentalities, gorgeous, Toni Tandalayo." I couldn't imagine writing a book about my modeling days without including some of Toni's stories, so I asked her if I could interview her. This was in 1975. She gave me an enthusiastic "Yes!", and when I arrived at her house for the interview, she answered the door nude.

Something about the way Toni looked and carried herself had a dramatic effect on people, wherever she went, according to Toni, even at gas stations and tollbooths. "Sometimes, the people get so excited they don't even fill up my tank and they charge me for a full tank." "Many times, they fill up the tank and they don't charge any money at all. That's just how excited they get and when I'm going across the bridges, I don't have to pay a lotta times. They just be looking at me and they don't take the money and they just be flabbergasted, and they just stare at me. When I go out to eat sometimes, they always watch me, and when I'm going anyplace, I get looked at. Many people have gone with me, like my sisters and friends, and people always turn around and stare and nearly have accidents looking at me and watching me."

One afternoon, Toni told me, some workers showed up to paint the outside of the school where she was modeling. She said one of the painters was especially taken with her. "I guess I must have been the most beautifulest thing he'd ever seen," she told me. The next morning, the man showed up drunk at work. "I imagine he did that so early in the morning because he wanted to feel that he could look without feeling guilty. You know how some people are about art." The painter chose a place to work that was just outside a high window looking into the room where Toni was modeling. From where she was posing on the stand, she faced directly toward the window. She could see "even without moving [her] eyes—a good model tries not to do that"—She said she could see that the man "wasn't doin' what he was supposed to be." He was looking through the window at her, and she could tell he thought he was getting away with something.

Suddenly, the painter lost his balance and fell. She learned later that he had fallen to his death. The story ended up in the newspapers and on the TV news. "I didn't ever tell anybody what really happened," Toni said. "They investigated and whatever. Well, I didn't have anything to say or do. The poor fellow was just enjoying himself and the beauty of my modeling, and uh, he just happened to lose his balance. He might have felt that by my pose being over and I was looking his way, he wouldn't want me to catch him looking, so that's when he lost his balance and fell to his death."

Her Song
Nancy Gotthart

TONI'S WORK ETHIC

I asked Toni if anything ever "bad" had happened to her during her modeling career. Then she told me that one day just before she was supposed to model for a class, she was raped. "It was a terrible experience," she told me. "I never had anything like it. I was beaten on the face and my body was sore." She showed up at the class anyway. The teacher, Mr. Beates, was someone she often worked for. "I was a little late and that was about all," she said. "I explained to Mr. B. what happened, and he understood." Right after that class, she went on to do a couple of other jobs. "You can rely on me and you can depend on me," she said. "I didn't want to let anything interfere with my modeling."

When Toni told me her stories about being raped and almost being raped, I felt very sad. I couldn't help but remember an experience I had when I was traveling in Greece. I had met four Canadian women at a hostel in Rome. They invited me to come along with them to Crete. I think they wanted me to share the cost of the gas in the car they were going to rent and food.

We had to take an overnight ferry boat. It was a large ferry with bunks for men and women to sleep on the bottom deck. The five of us were in the back of the first row of bunk beds. Since they were friends and there were four bunk beds together, they got first dibs. I slept alone in the bunk bed at the very end. The bunk bed opposite me was empty. I got into my sleeping bag, got out the book I was reading (*The Caucasian First Circle*), and curled over on my side facing the wall. I was deeply engrossed in the book, when I heard a noise directly opposite me. I turned and saw a man motioning to me if it was okay if he slept in the bed opposite me. I wasn't thinking clearly. I simply nodded "yes". It didn't occur to me to wonder what he was doing on the women's side or how he got there. I continued reading.

Within minutes, I felt a scratching on my sleeping bag near my head. As I turned, I faced his penis ejaculating on me. I screamed. The young Canadian women leaned out of their beds, looking to see why I had screamed. All at once, a guard of some sort came down our aisle, took the man, who had his shoes in his hands, and motioned for me to follow. I think, I was in shock. Elaine, one of the young women I was traveling with, offered to go with me to the captain and tell him what had happened. I put on my glasses and my shoes. Elaine held onto my arm, as we tried to follow the sailor who was walking very fast onto the deck and up some stairs. The ship was tossing and turning, and it was nighttime, so even though I had my glasses on, I couldn't see very well.

As we entered what I guess were the captain's quarters, it was very brightly lit. The captain was awaiting me, pen and paper in hand. There were several sailors behind him unsuccessfully trying to hide their grins. The captain was also smirking. The man, whom I now saw was surprisingly handsome, was standing off to the side of the captain. In broken English, the captain asked me to tell him what happened. I couldn't talk. Elaine, then, with her big, blue eyes, turned-up nose, and innocent face, looked at the captain, grabbing my elbow harder, said, "He got the bed wet. Get it?" When I heard that, it was all I could do not to laugh. It just seemed so ludicrous that all this was happening and her description was an eye roller, even though I was mortified.

At this point, the man turned to me, put his two hands together, as if handcuffed, and said in perfect English, "Thanks to you, miss, I get 20 years in jail." Being who I was, I felt bad for him. Twenty years sounded like a long time. I looked over at the captain, who was saying, "Do you want to press charges, miss?" He still had a small smile on his face. Elaine was squeezing my arm even harder by this time. I blurted out, "No. Just tell him to read dirty magazines instead." The sailors looked like they didn't understand what I said, but the captain did. He motioned for the sailor to take us back to our bunks. I didn't look at the man. We followed the sailor again and felt the eyes of many women dressed all in black staring at us as we entered the women's side.

I slipped into my sleeping bag, unable to sleep or read. There were lightbulbs swinging from the ceiling every few feet and a sailor had been commanded to walk up and down our aisle all night long.

At one point, I did fall asleep, but when I heard the sailor's footsteps near my bed, I woke up and screamed again. He never returned.

Several hours later, the sun came up and we disembarked. It was apparent that the word got out all over the ship about the American "whore". Or, at least that's what I assumed they were thinking as I saw the women in black with their crosses staring at me as I walked down the plank and onto land with my head down.

If I had to go to a modeling job after that, I know I couldn't have. Toni blew my mind and brought back that experience.

I continued to interview her. She told me that one day, her period started while she was modeling for a class of all women with a male instructor. The students were thoroughly engaged with their work, and she was so determined to be a good model for them that she didn't stop posing, even when she noticed that something was going on with her body. "They were in it so good and so heavy, I hypnotized myself," she said. "I had feelings, but I didn't know that it was coming down so terrible heavy just as if I was havin' a miscarriage." The students must have noticed her blood flowing, but they didn't say anything, and they didn't stop working. "They kept going," Toni said. "I didn't know what to do. I didn't know if they would think I was a bad model if I stopped. So, I kept goin' on 'til the end of the pose. That was very unusual. They didn't ever say anything to me, but I was most embarrassed."

MIND POWER

The thing about Toni that struck me was that no matter what bad things might have happened, she was able to change her mindset to the positive.

Toni went on to say, "I know I told you a story about being raped before a booking, but another time I got to use my mind power to avoid it. Once a guy came right out of school and wanted to rape me. This was in the daytime right after noon. My car was parked right in front of the school, and I ran and got inside of the car before he could catch me, but before I got the door open, he wanted to rape me right on the sidewalk and then he got into the car and wanted to rape me right in the car, but I used this power that I have and talked him off. He went on his way."

Toni relied on her intuition a lot when she worked and used the power of her mind to make her modeling experiences go well. "I don't do anything without being true to my vibes," she said. "I listen to the inner me speaking. There is something that's within that I do believe in, and I really obey it. I don't let bad vibes get me down. When they send me to those new jobs, in order to keep from being fearful and become a failure, which always happens when you are afraid, I always send lots of love to the new clients and some good vibes. I say a little prayer which blesses them, and I praise them before I get there. It works. When I get there, they're no stranger to me and it's just exactly what I had hoped. They say I'm a good model and I do good work and they'd like to have me again. I just do that all the time."

She even used her mind to stay warm in a cold studio. "When I get cold, I never let anything bother me at all," she said. "We had a job over at the Fleisher building and they didn't have anything together yet. They had heaters, but no plugs, and it was really cold. So, I just turned on this inner imagination of heat that I have and worked right on. The teacher said I didn't have to bother about taking off my clothes if I didn't want to. I said, 'Well, I'll work nude,' and threw off my clothes. I said, 'If anyone wants to stay they can.' They stayed and I turned my heat on again and I worked. I worked full time, and everybody stayed the whole three hours without any problem at all."

She also used her mind to stay healthy. "I'm always positive about my health," she said, "and I never say that I'm going to catch this and catch that. People say, 'Haven't you had the flu? Or haven't you had this, or haven't you had that?' I say, 'No—I don't expect it and I don't accept it.' I tell it to get away if it starts to thinkin' it's going to come here: 'You don't belong here, and you'll get kicked out. I won't accept you in my life.'"

"I don't do anything without being true to my vibes. I listen to the uh, inner me speaking. There is something that's within that I do believe in and I really obey it. I don't let people's bad vibes get me down. I just uh, send mine out with more love to them, so they can help me to feel better up there."

She Could Have Danced All Night
Nancy Gotthart

TONI DANCING

"I get a chance to dance at schools sometimes," Toni told me. "I bring my own music, you know, when they want me to. I introduced this to them, and they liked it so well they started requesting me. Different classes would always let me dance and they'd always let me work out, you know, for the parties that they had. The last day of school they liked to give me special jobs because it was near the end of the class term and they wanted to all feel like it was a party, so they let me bring my music that day. They'd have food, wine and cheese, just like a party, and on Halloween, they merged several of the classes. When they didn't have a big enough room, they'd always get the auditorium and have me just dance like a big party. Everybody would come in and draw and just have a great time."

BREAKS

Toni said she tended to get so absorbed in the work that she didn't usually take advantage of the coffee and bathroom breaks the class instructors provided. She told me about one job where this could have caused a problem if not for her mind power. "I was workin' and enjoyin' it so," she said, "I didn't know when break time came. I let mind power keep me from shitting up there on the stand. I was thankful when the pose was over and I just said, "Excuse me" and went on back to the bathroom. It took me a long time to shit: one hour. But it came all out, and I was okay. I told you, I didn't accept this sickness. I just shit."

LIQUIDS

Toni wanted to tell me about her attitude about liquids. She never liked to drink liquids on the job: "I'm Pisces, you know, and that's 'pissies.' I would go right just like these little dolls that we used to play with, and we'd put the water in, and it would go right on through. That's the way I would do if I drank water. It's what I always do, so I wouldn't drink anything unless I drink at night. I know that they don't pay you to go to the bathroom. I seldom eat very much while I'm working, too. I don't like to go to work on a full stomach. I know in dancing, that's how come I can be so energetic. It takes the energy away, you know if you eat. I don't take advantage of the coffee breaks too much because the more you drink and go on, the less you can hold your balance or your poses and so on, and I like to remain a good model."

TONI'S "PISSIN CUP"

For times when avoiding liquids didn't solve the problem, she had a solution: "I take a pissin' cup around with me all the time," she told me. "I just piss in my cup and piss in my car. I can control it. If it don't finish, I just cut it off. That's what models have to go through. We models do have that problem."

"One time," she said, "Celeste, another model from the Guild, and I were workin' at the same place. I was going out and she was going in. Celeste had been shopping or somethin'. She had a nice little bag stashed in the back of the room that they had back there. Celeste was ready to go on, but I went back in there and there was nothin' in there but Celeste's things. I was staying so long. I think Celeste thought I was bothering her things or somethin', but I had to piss and there was no bathroom in there and I had me a cup in my bag and I was back there pissin'. That was what was goin' on. I was doin' some good pissin'.

"In a job like this, I get up mostly at five o'clock in the mornin' in order to get across that bridge on time, especially if I have an 8 o'clock appointment. It takes all that time to get ready and I don't like to be late. You can't always go to the bathroom at the same time all the time. So, sometimes you don't have time in between, so I sends it back where it comes from. When I get home, I piss. I'm not allergic to my bathroom. People think that everything is peaches and cream, but that is one of the problems that models have because they do not pay you to go to the bathroom. They don't realize how early you've gotten up and how much trouble you've gone through to get to them and that's what really pisses me off when I see somebody that don't appreciate me. I like people to really appreciate me and my work because I know what I go through to get to them and I'm going to give them my best and I do all of this in order to give them my best. If I sat around here and wanted to go to the bathroom, I'd be late, and they'd be waiting for me all the time, but I sends it on back and let it wait."

NORFOLK, VIRGINIA

"I never did drink coffee nor smoke, Norfolk, Virginia. Do you know what that means? Well, I said it fast. It's a little joke that I always say to the people. It keeps them laughing. Every time I work, and they offer me a drink, coffee or something like that. I say no, "thank you. I don't drink, nor smoke, Norfolk, Virginia." It sounded like you don't even fuck. I say "no thank you" in a very nice way, so some people know me by that.

"Oh, Helene," Toni told me, "I'd just like to dedicate this little poem to you and also to the models in general, because I found that it has helped me my whole life, which I believe has helped me be the beautiful model and person that I am. The name of it is *To Be Kind*. I am one of the kindest persons that you will ever meet and if everyone had the patience and the kindness that I have they would never, never regret it and they'd always find that they'd succeed in whatever.

She recited this to me nude.

To Be Kind

Be kind to every livin' thing
Hurt not, nor wound, nor slay
A lastin' peace will reign over all
And gladden every day
The birds will gaily sing to you
Flowers will smiling nod
For every time that you are kind, You do an act of God.

LI

Boom Boom

I thought interviewing Boom Boom could be fun. When I interviewed him, he said he had been modeling since 1969. He told me he had come to San Francisco and needed a job that had flexibility and would give him time to do other things. (He was a very good photographer.) He didn't want a job that was repetitive, like going to the same place every day, because that would have driven him up the wall, and he liked the attention models get.

He said his first job was a big hassle because he had to hitchhike to the College of Arts and Crafts, on the other side of the Bay. He arrived nervous and late. He'd been in San Francisco for just a few months, and it was getting towards summertime. Wanting to get a suntan, he had gone up to the rooftop of the building in which he lived and put baby oil all over himself, while he basked in the sun, nude. He stayed out too long and got what he called a "marvelous" sunburn on his cock and balls which started to swell up until they looked like a "Mr. Natural" drawing. They were also very itchy. He was embarrassed, but nobody said anything, and nobody got red in the face or tittered, so he supposed that they thought he had a two-foot dong all the time.

To David, the worst thing about modeling was not having enough money. His pet peeve, though, was having "dumb" teachers who let their classes get into petty gossiping, rather than drawing. He liked it when the teacher was "real strict." He found it amusing if the students were uncomfortable with the rules. He also would get very pissed off with students who continued to smoke when he asked them not to.

I asked him how he felt about working with other models. He replied that, ideally, he would like to work with someone about every third time. He thought sharing a job made it a lot easier and more fun, because you could gossip with the other model. "However," he said, "it had to be someone you could get along with because modeling with someone you don't like is a pain in the ass."

He told me about one time when he was working with a female model, and he somehow touched her leg. She thought he had tickled her, and she slapped him on the wrist. He got so royally pissed at her, that he didn't speak to her for the rest of the day.

David likes to have music when he works, except for trashy radio. He prefers to work for students who are interested in their work.

When I asked what he thought a good model was, he said that because he didn't draw, it was hard for him to say, but he would want to draw the "hunkiest." He would like to draw a model who did a variety of energetic, dynamic poses and long ones that were interesting visually, but very relaxed. A bad model, according to David, would be someone who's not feeling right about being there.

He recounted a time at the College of Arts and Crafts, when the teacher wanted to tie a bunch of bananas on him and then pick them off. I asked him where the bananas were tied. His crotch. He said he let her do it once or twice, but it wasn't very comfortable because the string she had wasn't very good. This was the '70s, when there were a lot of "happenings" taking place.

The teacher asked the models to go up to the loft and start throwing things, like pieces of paper at the students. There were about four models at this time doing it. He really got off on that.

He hated it when little kids would inadvertently see the model. When he worked at Woodrow Wilson High School, the window shades didn't quite close, and the kids would come by and heckle. The teacher used to run around with masking tape trying to cover up the holes.

If there were weird students in the class, he didn't necessarily mind them, unless their presence seemed jarring. If they could manage to blend in with the class, then he thought it was fine, although he was very curious as to who they were.

He said the students always asked him if he himself was an artist. I knew him to be a rather good photographer. On his breaks, he liked to talk to the hunky guys who turned him on and some of the ladies who were real appreciative. He thought the women were fine, unless they got in the way when he was talking to a hunky guy.

He said that for him as a gay man, working with women was like working with his mother or sister. Working with a guy, for him, can be embarrassing or great because of the sexual tension. He said if he felt that he was about to get an erection, he would think of the times he went swimming at Devil's Slide in 68 degree water and all his nether parts would shrivel up to two inches. That usually worked.

If any students propositioned him, he didn't pay much attention to them. He found it easier to relate to the other models, than the students.

Students gave him drawings. Sometimes he was very thankful and other times he was embarrassed. He kept them for a certain amount of time and then tossed them. A student once gave him a drawing that made him look like a boy version of a Vargas girl, which he said was his own fault because the guy had put some fabrics on the wall with wild Matisse sort of things on them. David remarked that it looked good. At the end of class, the guy gave him the awful drawing. David said his "psychological" face fell on the floor as he thanked him and left.

When he got cold, he'd make love to the space heater by getting as close as possible. If that didn't work, he'd simply put his clothes back on. David told me he sometimes liked to work with his clothes on because of the variety and breaking of the routine.

When I asked him if he ever was asked to do weird poses, he said there was an instructor once who wanted him to look as if he was humping the female model he was working with. He declined, saying he didn't feel comfortable doing that. The instructor backed off after that.

Another time at Sacramento State College an instructor had David, Katy and Tiny Merille working for him in a body-painting class. The instructor had all three models place themselves in front of the entire student body of about 200 people while the students in his class body painted all three during a noon assembly. David was livid. He said for a long time he couldn't stand that teacher's guts.

Then, he told me about a teacher who gave him a ride to class and proceeded to ask him what kind of poses he thought he would do that night. He just laughed in her face. He said to me, "Honestly, did she think I was going to waste my time figuring out what I was going to do in that dumb class? Really?" This is sort of like asking an excellent visual artist what she's going to paint that day.

His favorite place to model was outdoors, as long as there weren't any mosquitos or flies. He liked the bright sunshine with grass to sit on, although when he thought about it, he would prefer to sit on a rug on the grass. He preferred it to be a place where he could do reclining poses or swinging off of trees or bars, something in that order. He really liked it when a class had a rope hanging down or a pillar. If it was outside, as far as he was concerned, it could last all day with a break for lunch and maybe a few hours in the shade. Of course, his ideal class would have hunky men in it and all the ladies would be dykes and entertain each other. For lunch, David said, "There would be a big bacchanal and there would be really good artists who were into their drawings. Their work would be a wonder to look at and they would be interesting people."

David's idea of the worst class would be outside in the middle of a public square, no privacy, no heat, hecklers, lousy artists who not only couldn't draw but didn't care either, and a despondent, inattentive teacher who would rather gossip with the students for half the class, spending the time tittering with just one person.

When I asked him if he'd ever fallen down, he said that at the College of Arts and Crafts they had put him on a chair that was on top of a table or a desk because for some reason, they didn't have a modeling stand. It was a 3-hour pose, uninterrupted, because at that time he wasn't in the Guild and didn't know about taking breaks. When he finally got up, his leg was completely asleep, which made him not only fall off the chair, but off the table and onto the floor.

His favorite poses are classical, statuesque kinds of poses, like Roman or Grecian statuary or like Renaissance paintings.

I can't finish with David unless I tell you that I used to model with him on occasion. For some reason, that I can't remember, his nickname was Boom Boom. Boom Boom and I would be in a pose together and he would whisper in my ear about a "hunky" guy that both of us were checking out. *A lot of fun.* Boom Boom was wicked. Once, he decided to be even more wicked than usual. We were working together, and I was in a seated pose. He was standing over me and had my wrists in his hands. He positioned himself so that if he just slightly moved his hands, my breasts would jiggle. "Stop it!" I said under my breath. He looked at me with his smiling beady eyes and whispered, "No." Fucker. He kept up the jiggling throughout the 5- minute pose. *Grrr.*

THE THREE-WAY

One sunny afternoon in San Francisco, Boom Boom and Eduard (a stunningly gorgeous model from the Guild who was part Japanese and part German) and I decided to try and do a three-way on the roof of Boom Boom's apartment building. Why? I honestly don't know. Both Eduard and Boom Boom were gay. When we got to the roof, we spread out some blankets and disrobed. Looking out over the rooftops of the buildings, we could see in the city. It took a while for us to even look at each other. When we finally did, I think it was Boom Boom who said, "Um. I'm not feeling it."

Eduard added,

"No, neither am I."

And then I nodded in agreement. At this, we three nude models burst into guffaws, put our clothes back on, grabbed our blankets and made our way back down into Boom Boom's apartment.

LII

Poems about Modeling

I asked Carla Christman from the Model's Guild if she would be willing to be interviewed for the book. Her response was, "I'll just send you a couple of poems."

MODELING ON SATURDAY AFTERNOON
BY CARLA CHRISTMAN

Saturday booking,
Working with the weeks
tired wrapped around me.
From the window
I watch the rich man's regatta on
the bay,
see the flat-footed march of
seagulls

on the neighboring
red tile roof.
The timer ticks away my
weekend in twenty-minute
segments.

THE MODEL

BY CARLA CHRISTMAN

Old men take forever to set up their easels, sharpen pencils, locate charcoal. And then they draw their fantasies, making you years younger with thighs the likes of which you've never seen.

Girls and younger women are cruel.

They hold the Conte crayon like razor blades to hack lines deep into your face, and draw the droop of breasts with merciless accuracy.

Older women dab, delicate watercolors. Their own lost youth and sex reflected in your painted eyes. They are the last to leave, rolling up their sadness like canvas.

Gay men draw whatever's there. They don't care.

LIII

Contemporary Artist Model Interview 2021

Griselda

Griselda is a current model in Santa Cruz. She started modeling in Miami. When I asked her what her main complaints were, if any, she said, "People try to talk to you afterwards when they see you nude. They try to ask you out. Like, 'what do you do on the weekends?' Nothing. 'Want coffee?' No. 'Beer?' I don't drink."

Art students would buy her food from the cafeteria at Miami International University, and she would let them. The food was terrible, "But a girl's gotta eat," she said. Griselda is also an artist. That's what she does for a living.

She told me about a model she absolutely adored. "There was an amazing model...a Yugoslavian woman, named Bezna, probably around 67 years old. She was just a hustler. She was a dumpster diver, and she would adopt stray dogs and had a very thick accent.

"Oh, you do not believe vat people throw in garbage. I find puppy in garbage...Corgi is such good dog."

Griselda loved her because she had folds and texture and had a really cool body to sculpt, better than the conventionally beautiful body.

Griselda went on to say that there was an animation program in Miami, and those students were the most creepy. "They were inappropriate, socially awkward and had never experienced a nude lady in the room. They were not chill." She said the women students were never a problem. "Not even the gay girls ever. Just the boys."

Griselda said she used to scandalize her professors with her body of artwork, a series of erotic paintings, especially one of her professors who was very conservative, a mid-Western teacher. There was a lesbian in the class where all her work was about cunnilingus. The professor was flustered and didn't like it. He loved puppy drawings. Those drawings got better grades. *Barf.*

She told me then that she had entered a very inappropriate relationship with a much older man in Santa Cruz. She said that he liked that she called him 'Daddy'.

The first time she met *Daddy* was the day she and her mom walked into his sculpture studio. His art was incredibly beautiful. She told her mother that he made beautiful women in bondage straps. Her mother then said to him, "Oh Griselda has a bunch of these in her closet."

Her mother was super naïve and didn't really know what those were." She said she just thought, *Oh, God.*

His jaw dropped like a Tex Avery wolf. He was instantly upset. She said, "Shut up, Mom. Don't out me."

Then, she said, the guy was suddenly like, "I must sculpt you."

She didn't start modeling for him right away until she had started dating him at her mother's insistence, saying, "He's such a catch." He was in between her mother's age and hers. She asked her mother why she didn't just date him, feeling repelled. Her mother told her to try it out.

She ended up negotiating with him for a workspace because she liked sculpting. She started assisting in his studio which was a great opportunity. She got to work the kilns and liked being physical and strong, lifting heavy things. She said her body was never in better shape. Then, she agreed to be sculpted.

He did a life-sized ceramic sculpture. It had three wolves and she was going to be a warrior woman. But soon, he started becoming very possessive of her. She told me he was too obsessed. She started feeling like the younger chick and arm candy. It started getting really weird because he got jealous when her artwork was more appreciated than his, and he was famous.

She said that when a guy showed up to Open Studios in Santa Cruz and was taken away by her work and not paying attention to "Mr. Sculptor", he was livid.

He was pissed off that he was the one who owned the studio, and the person was more taken with her work. A screaming fight followed. She told me she should have broken up with him then, but she didn't. That was the first sign of weird insecurity issues, and it started getting progressively worse.

Eventually, she just grabbed all her stuff and got out of there. The whole inflated artist ego just didn't work. She said, "I'd prefer to struggle."

She told me she tended to go for "farming, hippy boys who grew plants and were free, living off the land and didn't have their shit together. The famous sculptor seemed to have a career, a reputation, a name and her mother was impressed.

This is why she doesn't date artists any more.

LIV

A Few Art Teachers' Stories

Death and Life

Thinking about different perspectives, I realized that I hadn't really interviewed any art teachers. When I was in Costco (I go every week, like an idiot) I ran into a couple I know from both the thespian and art world. Lillian Bogovich is one of the finest actors in Santa Cruz and her partner is a well known artist and teacher in the community. I told them about my memoir. Mark immediately said, "Oh, I could tell you stories!" I took him up on it.

While Mark Levy was an art student in college, they had normal life models on a regular basis in a semester long class, several times a week. On one occasion, the instructor had arranged for the students to go to the department where they had corpses. Other than his grandfather, Mark had never seen a dead person.

So, the students and the teacher went into the room where the dead bodies were stored. They were on aluminum gurneys with the covers off, and the female corpse was all wrapped in gauze and soaked in formaldehyde. The professor unwrapped the gauze. She was probably 60 something, and they proceeded to draw her. Part of her abdomen had been opened up, exposing organs. He closed it up and later opened it, so they could draw it. But what surprised him most was that after one dies, apparently the fingernails continue to grow, as does the hair (her grey roots were showing).

This was the late '60s, early '70s. Mark told me that none of them were affected adversely by the idea or the smell of death. The fascination overruled any squeamishness. She was their model. It felt to him like she was the one paying because they were drawing her after she had passed.

He told me another story about a model named Wendy who had been their model at Cabrillo, the local community college. He said that he and she had gotten to know each other outside of class. She modeled around Santa Cruz. She worked at the Art League and Angelo Grova's studios. Wendy was interested in ceramics, and Mark was a ceramic teacher at Santa Cruz High. He was the chair of the art department. He had built a large facility with raku firings and vaper kilns.

Wendy wanted to know if she could volunteer in the classroom in exchange for being able to use the facility. She did that for at least a year and through the nine months of her pregnancy.

Mark had been doing a lot of plaster casts of torsos a la George Segal, an internationally famous painter and sculptor in the pop art movement. A week before Wendy was ready to give birth, she was just glowing and asked Mark to make a plaster cast of her pregnant torso. Fourteen years later, Daphne Moon, her daughter, took his class at Santa Cruz High. He had the plaster negative of her mother stored in the back room of the ceramic studio.

A few months into the semester, he had figured out who Daphne, (Wendy's daughter) was. So, one day while she was on the opposite end of the studio and couldn't see what Mark was doing, he put the plaster cast on her work table and walked away. When she came back to her work table, he went to the opposite side of the room and proceeded to observe.

Daphne sat down and asked her girlfriend sitting next to her, "What's this?" Her girlfriend said, "I don't know. Mr. Levy just put this here and walked away." Daphne looked puzzled. It was the life-sized negative of her mother, a week before delivery. After just looking at it and looking around the room to see where Mark was, suddenly, her eyes got huge and she said, "Oh my God! That's me!" Daphne looked over at him. "This is me inside my mom, before she gave birth to me." He eventually came over and suggested she press some clay into it and make a positive of it. I asked Mark about this because I know nothing about sculpture in that regard. He told me that until clay is put onto the frame and fired, it is called a negative.

Then he told me about a time when he was in college at Long Beach State. They had the largest underground foundry in the Western Hemisphere. He said they had a male model, and the professor was talking to the students between poses. Mark said there must have been some attractive or stimulating students in the classroom because the model got a hard on. The professor, without missing a beat, with the model on his side, turned, whacked him on his dick with a pencil, and kept on talking as the boner deflated quickly. Everyone laughed, except perhaps the model and the best part was that it was almost as if nothing unusual had just happened and he kept on giving his lecture.

LV

Speedo or Not?

Besides being a ceramicist, painter, model and dog walker, Diane Margiotta also taught art in a private high school on the East Coast for over 30 years. She said that although it was an all-girls school, the boys from a neighboring school were allowed to attend certain classes, so the students could have the co-ed experience.

Diane was teaching an art class in which she hired two models, a male and a female. Since it was a high school class, she sent home a note for parents to sign saying it was okay for their son or daughter to draw the nude. She said she would have the male model put on a Speedo.

There was only one student whose parents objected. Diane said they were a Catholic family, and that she had never known any other Catholics to object to something like this. The agreement was that the daughter could draw her friend if the friend wore a leotard. That was the way for her to do the assignment.

The middle school teachers got word of what Diane was doing and voiced objection to the male model having to cover up in a

Speedo and the female model not. Diane put an end to that discussion by asking them if they would like to answer the calls from the parents. She also said that she explained that men's anatomy, in case those teachers weren't aware, was different from a female's. There might be more "issues" with a man than a woman. She went further to say that the particular male model was very muscly and that the students didn't need to draw "noodles."

Another story Diane mentioned was when her class was opened to include male students from the neighboring high school and only one came. She said he did a particularly beautiful drawing of the female model for which he received a lot of praise. Things turned mysterious when his drawing suddenly was nowhere to be found. To this day, Diane never found out what happened to it.

LVI

Linda Levy's Nasty Stories

When I told Mark Levy that I thought I could use a few more stories from an artist or instructor's point of view, he asked me if I knew Linda Levy. I did not. He told me that she was a kick in the pants and proceeded to call her to ask if she'd be willing to give me a few stories. She was more than willing. In fact, she wanted to tell me immediately on the phone, but I was too spent having interviewed Mark for a couple of hours. I called her a few days later, and she gave me an earful.

One of her stories was about the first time she substituted at Cabrillo College in Aptos, California for a life drawing class. She was in her twenties then and not very experienced as an instructor. She was subbing for Howard Ikemoto, a brilliant artist and well-respected instructor.

There was a male model. During his longer pose, he got an erection. She said, "That happens. It's a long pose." -- but he actually came. *Gross.* The class was stunned. The model didn't react in any way.

Linda wasn't going to make a big deal about it during class, but afterwards, she told the model that it wasn't cool and that he had to control himself. He didn't give a shit. "Somebody like that probably gets off on people looking at him," she guessed.

After the class, Linda recommended to Howard that they don't rehire this model. Howard was only upset by the fact that he got the new blanket soiled.

Another story she told me was when she led a class at Cabrillo, the model undressed, and the model had one of her nipples pierced with an enormous amount of junk hanging off of it, as if it were a keychain with a lot of crap on it.

Linda went on to say that when the model disrobed and started to pose, a few people gasped, and then, there was dead silence. Soon, a little voice piped up and said, "I have to know. I have to ask. Does it hurt?" Linda started laughing along with the rest of the class.

When I asked her what the model's response was, she said the model grinned, but didn't say anything. Linda blurted out to me, "She didn't say anything, like this is the key to start the car or anything like that." *Groan.*

Linda told me that she can always tell when a model is inexperienced. She has a method to get them to relax that usually works. What she has them do is a series of 60-second poses. (These are actually my favorite. I get to be creative with movement and get a lot of exercise.) It just didn't seem to be working with this one male model. So, she tried another technique.

She asked him, "Do you do yoga, dance, or stretch exercises before you run or something?" He didn't do any of them. He was stiff as a board with his arms at his side. So, she started throwing things at him, had him catch them, and hold. This seemed to do the trick. "Pretty imaginative, if you ask me!" she bragged.

Linda told me that she doesn't let students use erasers in her class, but she happened to have a few in her hand, having taken them away from sneaky students. She beaned the model with the erasers, which caused him to twist and turn, which is what he needed to do. She does the same thing with 2B pencils. *Just visualizing this is hysterical.*

She said that after a few life drawing classes, that male model actually loosened up and learned how to pose.

Linda went on to tell me about another model. This one was a belly dancer and kept moving her hips. That did not work. In drawing classes, the poses are usually 5 to 10 minutes. One doesn't move during the pose. *Ahem.*

Over the years, Linda has worked with more than a few women who want to be drawn. Once, there was a very pregnant one, who started doing yoga stretches. Linda thought the baby was going pop out right then. Linda drew her and the model purchased the final piece. She entitled it *Great Expectations.*

Linda told me she always tried to get a male model at least once or twice a month for a workshop she was teaching at the Tannery in Santa Cruz. She had heard about a male model who was really good. She finally got a hold of him. He had a powerful upper body. He kept going to the back of the screen she had set up for the models to change behind, which she thought was odd. She soon discovered he was stroking himself, so he would look partially erect. She made the decision; she didn't want him back.

When the students asked her why he wasn't coming back, she said she didn't appreciate what he was doing behind the screen. Some of the female students wanted him back however. *Go figure.*

Linda went on to tell me about more male models. She said there once was a model who had really large testicles, and he would place them forward. They were large and red. (that reminded me of Boom Boom when he got a sunburn on the roof of his building in SF) She wanted to ask him what was wrong. She said he would bring instruments and play a saxophone. That part was unique as well.

She told me about another uncomfortable experience she had with a model when she was in her fifties. She said they had a male model who was well-developed and did great poses. She said he knew how to move, even his hands. Linda realized at one point that he was coming on to her. She didn't recognize that readily. She was totally surprised and taken aback, but even though she liked him as a model, she didn't want to encourage him. It was shocking and flattering. She was a little blind-sided. She told me that at her age, and being married, it just never occurred to her that a model would be interested in her in that way.

It was around that time that some of the male students in the class were *inappropriate* with the models, so she wrote up some guidelines as to appropriate behavior in the classroom. Everyone had to read it and sign it. One rule was the artist never touched the model - ever, and no photos unless the model said "OK".

Linda's gotta say something; if she doesn't, then she feels she is condoning the behavior. So, she told me she would get pretty verbal.

A month after a particular event apparently, there were a couple of students who convinced the model to have an erection. This was not in her class.

A month later, Linda had the same class, and it was obvious that inappropriate behavior had transpired earlier. She had heard about it through one of the male students as it made him feel uncomfortable about the drawing session.

I asked Linda if she recalled any unusual setups for the model during her career as a teacher and an artist. She told me that one time the students convinced a model to pose up on a ladder. She said it was fun drawing this as they were great poses, but these days because of liability, it would not be a good idea.

The final story she told me was about a young gal who was new to modeling. She took Linda aside during one of her breaks and told her that she had been modeling and doing photographs, but the artist wanted her to have a shaved pubis and he wanted to do it himself. She asked Linda if this was normal and expected. Linda enlightened her that this was definitely not a part of modeling. She encouraged the young woman to stop working for this artist.

Listening to Mark and Linda was a good way for me to see the whole picture from an instructor's point of view.

LVII

Full Circle

Being A Judge

Years later I got to demonstrate for the Models Guild auditions. I told them I was writing a book about modeling. They said, if I demonstrated poses, I could be a judge. That was flattering. When I realized how many people would be watching me so closely, I began to get a little nervous. All the other judges told me the day would be boring and horribly exhausting. I didn't believe them. I looked forward to it in the same way I enjoyed studying the students in the art classes. There were 80 people trying out.

That day, I got to be one of the five ominous judges sitting in a row. What the Guild looked for in a model was an interesting looking person, who knew how to move his or her body and who would know not to stand on one leg with arms outstretched for a 3-hour pose. Ideally, this person should come in any shape or size. In fact, the Guild appreciated any digressions from the "American Ideal." Interestingly enough, although one may want to, models are not forced to retire at 65 years old.

It's also important that the models be responsible enough to get to work on time, to remember they have a job to get to, not to be rude or throw temper tantrums, and to be fairly hygienic. This sounds very basic, but these particular combinations were sometimes hard to find. It could be because, in the '70s, at least the pay was very low for artist models in California, and driving, hitchhiking or taking the bus all over the San Francisco Bay Area for an 18-hour work week can get to be quite tedious. Therefore, not only do the judges have to look at about 70-100 bodies in one day, but they also have to try to guess if these people were *together* enough not to endanger the Guild's reputation. Unfortunately, there were always a few hideous mistakes.

On the day I was working as a judge, the Guild board members and I went into a filthy room at the SF Art Institute. I don't know what this room is like now, but then, it was famous for its fleas on the model's stand. We began cleaning it up for the models. Then, we let in the first group of forty. Nancy, the booking agent, gave everyone a little talk about the Guild, just as she had done four years earlier when I auditioned, and Katy introduced me. I felt petrified all of a sudden, but my acting experience kicked in. I disrobed, did a few poses, put on my robe again and sat down. I was relieved that my part of the show was over.

We then sat down to watch the would-be models show us their poses, one by one. The voting members had to write down a brief description of each model, so we could remember them later when we discussed them. Each person would burst through the door (many shaking like a leaf), hand over a written resume and two dollars. If you were accepted, you got that amount subtracted from your initiation fee. I felt so sorry for them. The secretary would read off the important parts of their resume, and they would be asked to do examples of short and long poses. Even though I had been through this myself, I had forgotten how intense it all was. Right away, it became obvious who had actually worked as a model in the past and who had not. I realized that being a good artist model was truly an art form, not just anyone can do it. At those auditions we were only going to be able to accept four people.

Out of the 70 or so bodies, there were a few who stood out and not necessarily in a good way. There was one disgusting, repulsive man who had auditioned many times before. We recognized him and asked him to leave. He was told that there was no room for him in the Guild. That may sound cruel to you, but I recognized him from when I modeled in Los Angeles. More than once, when I was on the model's stand, he would walk into the room, disrobe and try to get on the stand with me. It was really sad and a bit scary. He could hardly walk, his hands shook, and he used a cane. His face looked tired and needy, and his eyes weren't focused. He told everyone he lived with his mother and posed for pornographic magazines. He had photos of himself in an album in pornographic settings, which he would show to the instructors, begging them to let him model. He got pornography and art modeling confused. He continued to send the Guild letters with photos of himself in poses featuring his anus, with his telephone number and ads cut out with his name on them, like the stuff in the *Berkeley Barb* (a weekly underground newspaper during the '60s), begging to get into the Guild. He even called the Guild at 8 a.m. once, to tell Katy he'd seen her in a magazine. *Right.*

At the auditions that day, he was there with his protégé! A pathetic person actually wanted to follow in his footsteps. I remembered that guy from Los Angeles, too. He actually knew how to model though. His hero, Mr. Creepy, was handing out flyers of himself to the other models who were auditioning. These flyers had his name printed in big letters with his phone number. It said he would give massages and teach yoga techniques with a hint of kinky sex. *Um, no thank you.* When he walked in the door, he opined, "I've given out a hundred of these flyers and I haven't had one response. What could be the problem?" A model on the board said, "Maybe it's your approach." This one-liner got a burst of laughter, as you can imagine. His protégé was allowed to audition however.

Before the auditions, we judges were all given little pieces of gold paper, which we could use to flag each other in case of a real bozo creep. The gold paper meant "get rid of the asshole immediately." Needless to say, within 30 seconds of the protégé, there were six pieces of gold paper in full view with the same six people looking down at their notes or up at the ceiling. To give you an example of what he did, the secretary didn't even get a chance to read his resume before he bolted down to the floor, so close that he was almost touching us and started giving us these gross shots of his asshole, meanwhile managing to have a tortured, crazy man's look on his face. The last thing any one of us wanted to see was his anus. His face was bad enough. He may as well have been frothing at the mouth.

We were so stunned that Katy forgot to stop him and I final poked her. Worst of all, besides his attitude, was his odor. You can only imagine. Although, I wouldn't recommend it. This may sound harsh to you, but I had to build up a pretty good defense system at that moment in order not to scream. I think he got to do three poses and was told as politely as possible that we'd seen enough.

Then followed an exact opposite, yet equally unnerving experience. There were three real beauties who tried out, one after the other. The first young woman had jet-black hair and green eyes. The second was a redhead with long wavy hair, startling blue eyes and alabaster skin. The third was an African-American with a perfectly formed fro and a sassy attitude. They were so very beautiful, that I don't think anyone would have been able to concentrate on whether or not they were good models. We all were so turned on by them, simultaneously blushing and giggling. You could hardly ask them any questions really. All we could do was just basically stare and pant. I kept crossing and squeezing my legs. Katy's face at one point was as red as a petunia. Nancy was grinning. Other models, like Boom Boom, were chortling. John was laughing. Celeste and the woman from the Art Institute were staring.

After the combination of the earlier creep and those three beauties, it took all of us about three more models to be able to get back to normal. I kept feeling guilty about how unfair this was, and then I remembered back to my actress days, when I had been rejected countless times after auditioning. I had felt my life depended upon the reactions of the directors or agents, and often was so insecure, I blew it. I was hoping that being on the other end of auditions would make me feel good, but I felt awful.

I realized that I was only human, and I couldn't help my reactions. If I was bored, turned on, or horrified, well, that's life. That was life when I was an actress too, except that I didn't realize then that the directors might have been human. I suppose the one thing wrong with auditions is something that my father had pointed out to me: "You never get any feedback on how you did, what they actually thought of you, and how you could possibly improve."

On the other hand, if those people were to have seen the descriptions of themselves that the judges jotted down, they might have been totally broken right there. Those quick notes were vicious at times. For instance, if you saw a note about yourself like, "pale, Charles Manson, tacky hippie body" or "threadbare snatch, lovely asshole" or "Wicked Witch of the West," you might want to drop dead at that point, but if we could just have written something on each postcard telling them that they did not get in and either they should get more experience or not try modeling, or that they were very good, but not the type we were looking for, something like that, which would be truthful and tactful, I think the auditions would have been less sadistic. There was one model who told me I had intimidated her by my poses. I was very flattered and also sorry, remembering how intimidated I was by Katy and Susan when I had auditioned.

I probably would have died a thousand deaths, if I had been told never to come back, that there wasn't room for me, but, then again, I would at least known where I stood. I couldn't lie to myself. So, in a way, the creepy guy was one of the lucky people at the auditions.

To be a judge is an emotionally draining experience. After looking at those bodies all day long, it became difficult to concentrate. The fact that there were so many people meant that we could only see them for about five minutes each. The auditions were not publicized, and yet all these people somehow found out and showed up. Of course, the small handful of space-cases managed to zap the energy out of the air.

One man who auditioned looked like he sold encyclopedias. I thought for a minute that he must be putting us on and perhaps was a dynamic model in disguise. Wrong. He left his socks and his black plastic glasses on, while taking stiff, awkward, encyclopedia-selling type poses while his eyes were bugged out to kingdom come. We looked down or sideways or anywhere but at him.

Not all the models who auditioned were that strange. Looking at good ones left us feeling exhilarated. By the end of the day, it was fairly clear who was in.

LVIII

Moving On

Meeting Husband #1

While I was living in the Bay Area and working for the Models Guild, I met the man who became my first husband. It's definitely a '70s kind of story. My housemate in Oakland was sleeping with a woman who was in an open relationship with a guy I was dating. (Yep. You might have to read that sentence more than once.) She was a screamer, and I didn't enjoy listening to her. On one particular night, I decided that I'd had enough and decided to sleep at the home of my girlfriend Kristen, a seamstress who, as it happens, sewed some way cool outfits for the late harmonica-playing, singer-songwriter Norton Buffalo, aka Phillip Jackson. I grabbed my sleeping bag and set out to the house where Kristen lived with a few housemates. I was on the floor in the living room, mostly asleep, when one of the housemates opened the front door. He was wearing a karate gi. When he saw me on the floor, he began a Robin Williams-style, non-stop monologue about why he couldn't possibly sleep with me because he had to put in a sprinkler system in the morning. I was very amused, of course, because not only did I not know him, I had no intention of sleeping with him.

At the end of his monologue, he said, "So, would you sleep with me?" I said, "Yeah, sure." I'm not sure why I said "yes" exactly; I think basically for the adventure of it.

The man's name was Richard. After that chance encounter, we embarked on a six year relationship. After the first three years, his grandparents insisted we no longer "live in sin" and wanted us to get married. He loved his grandparents. (His father was an asshole and his mother was sweet and suffering.) His grandfather was a kick. He once said to Richard, "If you can't find it, put some hair around it and you'll find it." He actually had a fatal heart attack at my parents' house in Big Sur.

We rushed him to the hospital in Carmel, but it takes an hour to get there, and it was too late.

When Richard's grandparents urged us to get married, in the spirit of the times, we thought, "Okay, why not? We can always get divorced." We lasted three more years. I did learn Tae Kwon Do during that time. Richard was a second-dan (rank) black belt.

We first moved to New Monterey, California, in 1975 and lived there for about a year. Then he and I moved to Santa Cruz, California. This place that has the ocean and the forest and people who, for the most part, have open minds is where I have called home since 1976. I don't feel frantic here, at least most of the time. When I began writing this book in 1975, I wondered if I'd ever find another art form as satisfying as modeling. Well, I have: writing. Life is funny that way. I did return to theatre. I've been acting, directing and even writing plays. But this time, I don't feel competitive. Theatre is another art form. Being away from the ugliness that was Los Angeles during the late '60s, and being here allows me to participate in what I know best and enjoy.

I do miss modeling sometimes. The atmosphere of creativity in the air is a joy. I did mention to a friend of mine, who is a very talented painter, that I wouldn't mind modeling once in a while for her. She said to me, "Well, Helene, I would rather paint grapes than raisins!" I was tempted to show her that mine were not raisins, but I just put that statement in a poem instead.

ABOUT THE AUTHOR

Helene Simkin Jara is an award-winning author, actor, director and teacher. Her poems, stories, and plays have been published over 32 times.

In September 2020, Helene published her third book, *Turn Left at the Gorilla and Turn Down the Hall: and Other Stories*. This collection of short stories runs the gamut from humor to tragedy, taking the reader on a ride within the human and sometimes not so human experience. Her self-published first book *Because I Had To* was on Kindle's best-seller list in July 2014. She followed this success with her second book, *True Doll Stories We Remember*, an anthology of personal accounts of experiences with dolls. Helene's fourth book, *Life on The Stand*, is a memoir of her time working as an artist's model.

Helene is an active member of the Bay Area theatre scene. She is also a frequent collaborator with the podcast Coffee Contrails and Santa Cruz Actors Theatre.

To stay up to date on Helene's latest projects, be sure to follow her on Facebook, Instagram, and Twitter.

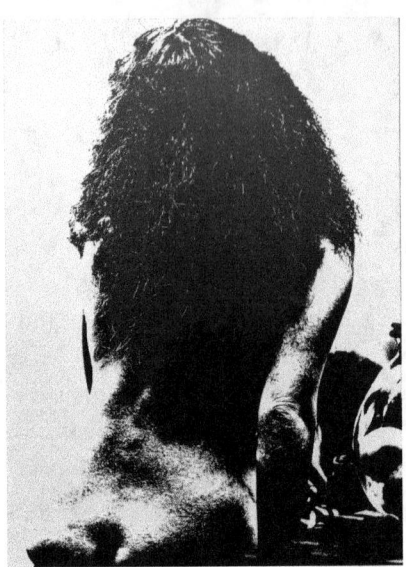

The End

Special Thanks!

Special thanks to the following people: Julia Huff, Nancy Gotthart, Linda Levy, Mark Levy, Toni Tondalayo, Carla Christman, Griselda, Norbert Schlaus, Diane Margiotta, Celeste Margiotta, Sarah Rabkin, Sharon Simkin Meinhoff, Karen Bell, Duke Houston, Gino Danna, Steve Kettmann

www.ingramcontent.com/pod-product-compliance
Lightning Source LLC
Chambersburg PA
CBHW071237070526
44583CB00017B/2217